Deep Into
Blue Holes

Deep Into

Blue Holes

The story of the Andros Project

ROBERT PALMER

UNWIN

HYMAN

LONDON SYDNEY WELLINGTON

First published in Great Britain by the Trade Division of Unwin Hyman
Limited, 1989

UNWIN HYMAN LIMITED
15–17 Broadwick Street,
London W1V 1FP

Allen & Unwin Australia Pty Ltd
8 Napier Street, North Sydney, NSW 2060, Australia

Allen & Unwin New Zealand Pty Ltd with the Port Nicholson Press
Compusales Building, 75 Ghuznee Street, Wellington, New Zealand

British Library Cataloguing in Publication Data

Palmer, Robert, 1951–
    Deep into blue holes: the story of the Andros project
1. Bahamas. Cave diving expeditions
I. Title
917.296'04

ISBN 0–04–440380–1

Designed by Julia Lilauwala
Photoset by Nene Phototypesetters Ltd, Northampton
Printed in Great Britain at the Cambridge University Press, Cambridge

*To Frank Martz, Archie Forfar
and Roberta Swicegood,
who explored too far and found
a different reward.*

Contents

Foreword by HRH The Duke of Kent   ix

Preface   xi

1   Rat Cay   1

2   Benjamin's early days   5

3   South Bight and the Wall   15

4   Conch Sound   35

5   The Inland Cenotes and Conch Sound Two   44

6   Doughnuts and disagreements   54

7   Stargate, Elvenhome and the Ocean Holes   73

8   The Andros Project: Avalon and Stargate   85

9   Elvenhome and El Dorado   101

10 El Dorado and beyond the limits of Stargate   112

11 Sanctuary   130

12 Porcupine Hole   143

Appendix I   Equipment   151

Appendix II Sponsorship   157

Index   161

Foreword

*F*OR the last seven years I have had the great pleasure of being associated as Patron with the British and International expeditions to the Blue Holes of Andros Island.

The success of these expeditions, working in one of the most hazardous environments faced by modern explorers, speaks highly of the dedication of their members to adventure and research on the underwater frontier. It is a measure of their commitment to safety and technique that these expeditions have been carried out without loss of life, or serious accident.

I share the hope of the divers that these caves will remain as special places, and that we, mankind, will not despoil them by careless misuse. I hope this book helps to convey to you some of the wonder that I felt on hearing of this unique world beneath the seas and islands of the Bahamas.

HRH The Duke of Kent

Preface

W E LIVE in a tired world. Its boundaries draw in, colours move on the maps, but the shapes stay the same. There are no monsters or mermaids drawn on the seas, the kraken sleeps, and the edges are too well defined.

What is left? There are great adventures to be had, journeys to be made, outside our planet. There are even, for a few dedicated travellers, corners of the surface that have been little visited, and still offer surprises. But someone's *been* there first. Too often these days 'expeditions' are mounted to retrace the footsteps of others who had better reason to be there in the first place, or to provide a vicarious thrill for fee-paying participants. Such 'expeditions' are really glorified holidays that create an aura of self-importance by use of the word. Dreams draw further away, we see television turn our fantasies into fabric, create heroes out of tinsel, and disguise the borders of the unknown behind a gloss of imagery. Earth may still be a beautiful creature, despite the worst we do to scar her, but she's an old friend now, no longer virgin.

But she still has hidden depths, and there are still those who dream real dreams. The explorations of the Blue Holes of Andros, over the past quarter-century, are far from over, and there are still rewards of original discovery for future explorers. Yet it would be a shame to think that their depths might be exploited for the casual thrill-seeker, the holidaymakers who have turned the slopes around Everest into a refuse heap, or who have beaten well-worn trails into the wild places of the planet, leaving them no longer wild. Exploration, all too often, is followed all too closely by exploitation. I would hope that our work will be the foundation of a conservation strategy for the protection of the wilderness beneath the Bahamas, not simply for a following crowd of financial exploiters and thrill-seekers, but that is up to the Government and inhabitants of the Bahamas to decide.

Underwater caves are dangerous places, and this alone should be enough to keep the cautious out. The caves themselves can take care of the most foolish, but the rest should treat them with the courtesy and respect that non-human life on our planet deserves and rarely gets.

I hope you enjoy this book, and that it satisfies your curiosity. I cannot claim credit for all of it, and there are many others who deserve a great degree of thanks; Dr George Benjamin, whose diaries provided much of the fabric of the first few chapters; his wife Hanni for much hospitality; his son George Junior; and Chris Howes, Bill Stone and Martyn Farr for help with the photographs. Many sponsors over the years helped make the story possible, and the most recent are acknowledged at the back of the book. To them, and to all the others who helped previously, many, many thanks. This is what happened . . .

Rob Palmer
St Briavels, 1988

CHAPTER ONE

Rat Cay

*A*T THE north-east end of the island of Andros, a kilometre or two offshore, sits a small islet with the unfortunate name of Rat Cay. Thick, scrubby bush straggles out of the low, coarse limestone ridge that forms the island, giving cover for the few birds and innumerable insects that inhabit it. The encircling sea, barely as deep as the island is high, conceals the beginnings of the complex and beautiful reef lying further offshore. A veritable confusion of marine life swims freely in and out of the coral heads, and lurks in the many-shaped hollows and crevices in between.

A deeper blue tints the sea on the northern shore of the islet. There, beneath the waves, a deep cleft splits the sea floor, a dark opening in the azure sands. Rich and colourful corals surround it, long waving hydroids fringe its walls, streaming to and fro in the strong currents that flow, sometimes in, sometimes out, of its depths. When the waters are calm, the cleft is a peaceful scene of tranquility, where shoals of fish float in studied laziness in the shadowed waters. Grunts and snappers inhabit the small maze of tunnels at the base of the cleft, multicoloured parrotfish chew enthusiastically at the coral, and the islet's resident barracuda casts a watchful eye over its domain. Occasionally a shark scatters the assembly, finning smoothly in to bask in the cool waters of the outflowing current.

At the foot of the cleft is a cave . . .

In the late 1960s, the opening at the western end of the cleft was one of those visited by a Canadian diver/photographer, Dr George Benjamin and his diving team, during their early explorations into the Blue Holes of Andros. George, a colourful and extrovert character who has never quite lost the Latvian accent of his original homeland, spent over twenty years visiting and cataloguing Blue Holes, exploring many of them for several hundred feet, occasionally to considerable depths. Rat Cay defeated him. Descending a shaft a few metres into the underwater cave, a short but roomy coral-encrusted passage led to a low, wide-bedding plane that proved too tight to enter with the bulky back-mounted tanks they were using. This narrow gap, 150 ft (45 m) from the entrance, and 55 ft (16.5 m) down, came to be regarded as the end of the cave, even though it was the source of a powerful current at the height of the tidal outflow. George moved else-where, and no one looked into the cave for a long time.

For several years, stories of the Andros Blue Holes circulated around the cave diving fraternity, exciting academic interest but little else. To most, they were the caves of the future; their depth, their remoteness, and their complexity put them beyond the range of existing techniques and experi-ence. But for a few, the lure became too great. The wheels of exploration were set into motion and, in 1981, an ambitious British diving expedition was launched.

Two years of painstaking and exhausting preparation, and an ageing DC3, brought me to Andros a few days ahead of the rest of the team. An American organization, International Field Studies of Columbus, Ohio, had offered us the use of their Forfar Field Station as our base, and it was from here one day early in my stay that their divemaster, Ken Jones, and his very attractive fiancée, Laurie, took me to Rat Cay to show me Benjamin's cave.

The years of preparation ripened to a personal fruition as I dropped over the side of the boat and, with Ken close behind me, swam into my first ocean Blue Hole. Down we fell, past the waving hydroids and gorgonians, past the skulking fish and their crustacean compatriots, and into the cleft. Unfamiliarity had brought us here at the height of the outflow, and this became only too apparent as we reached the inner pit. The fierce current pushed me back as I clawed my way down the rough, coral-encrusted walls, making lunges at likely projections until I could just look along the passage below, into the wide, low bedding. The clear, rushing current threatened to tear my mask from my face, but I could see enough to let me know that in calm water it would be passable. I opened my fingers and allowed the current to levitate me bodily up – and out! One more false start, with the waters flowing the other way, provided enough encouragement to bring us back with the full team.

We studied the currents, and their peculiar relationship to the tides on the surface, and got it right this time. Kitting up on the Forfars stations, we dived in and crossed the coral rim to the Blue Hole. The flow was almost non-existent, and the underwater visibility terrific. I sank slowly down the rift and passed the bedding with ease, my tanks slung on my sides on a special harness, that allowed me through where back-mounted tanks could not pass. Beyond the constriction I emerged into a large chamber, just as my line ran out. Fixing the end of the nylon cord to a half-buried block in the floor, I made a couple of short forays to establish the way on and, with wide eyes, looked 30–40 ft (9–12 m) straight down a large sand-floored passage, its walls graced with corals, sponges and anemones. Dozens of tiny red eyes gazed at me from a myriad crevices as a host of crawfish and shrimps took, in return, their first look at a cave diver. Martyn Farr arrived with a new reel, and followed me down the spectacular passage, past cowries grazing on the floor and the last silver snappers swimming upside down in blissful disorientation along the roof.

We passed an oxbow on the left. There, a passage split from the main tunnel only to rejoin it a few metres further on, where the skeletal remains of an incautious turtle lay half-buried in the sand. Here, at the end of the second reel of line, we made an exciting find. Swimming near one wall, regardless of our lights, were two true cave fish – *Lucifuga spelaeotes* – blind, pigmentless, and very cave-adapted. This pale and cryptic fish had only previously been recorded at three sites, all inland. This was our first marine sighting of the species, which had always been thought to be extremely rare. We swam back against a gathering current to decompress at the entrance, exhilarated by discovery. We had been where no other man had been before, a subaquatic, subterranean voyage of pure exploration.

Two days later we were back, this time with the Bahamian press in tow, looking for a story and somewhere to drink a crate of cold beer they happened to have found en route and brought with them. The outflowing current was still too strong to enter against, and we took a few photos around the entrance while we waited for the flow to drop. Eventually we became bored and, almost on principle with such an expectant audience, I clawed my way through the bedding against the final flow and set off to find virgin passage. The current was still very strong, and I had almost hit my air reserves as I tied a new reel on. In cave diving, a third of the air supply is used for going in, a third for going out, and a third saved for emergencies. My 'going in' supply was virtually finished, so physically hard had been the swim. Deciding, however, that going out would be rather fast, and would need little air, I pressed on down a steep, dramatic slope, past rock pendants and sand dunes to two huge collapsed blocks, framing the way on like two great megalithic dolmens. Martyn, having waited a few moments longer outside, now swam up to join me. Shortly beyond this point (which we called 'Heaven's Gate') the passage split into three, and became much smaller. I tied off and, low on air, sped out with the current to decompress with the fish while Martyn tried to progress a little further. He ran out a further couple of hundred feet of line, to bring the total length of our explorations to about 1,200 ft (360 m).

Was that it? Over the beers on the ride back, there was a nagging doubt, a lurking suspicion that we'd missed something. The flow at the end had lessened, and some must have taken another tunnel. We looked again.

Martyn tried again at the existing end, while I searched for side passages. Six hundred feet (180 m) from the entrance, on the right, I found a low sandy bedding which looked as though it might go. Carefully finning through the highest point – about 18 in (46 cm) from roof to floor – I struck a big, clean-swept passage, heading north. Gleefully, I ran out 300 ft (90 m) of line, to end the reel still in open cave. On my way back to the bedding, I discovered that some of the flow seemed to be going down impassable cracks in the floor, large enough for the shrimps that scuttered down them when I approached, but wide enough only for the smallest of Lilliputians to SCUBA into. Martyn, whose way on had become too low, was waiting back at the junction, and I scrawled a few notes on my slate – 'big passage, still going'. Martyn okayed and grinned, and went to see, adding another 200 ft (60 m) from his reel before he too ran low on air.

Our next push was our last. We came to a major roof collapse and, although I managed to wind my way through poised boulders for 30 ft (9 m) or so, it fast became too dangerous. We tried a smaller passage to the right of the choke, and made 200 ft (60 m) before it too became impassable. Silt billowed in the confined cave as we turned awkwardly round, and called it a day. Swimming back over the broken blocks of the collapse, we found them to be host to a profusion of tiny, delicate branching corals, translucently pink, and only a few centimetres high. This small colony of beauty was the only one of its type we found – another rare and colourful example of the wildlife of the caves. We called it the 'Rose Garden'.

There remained only one task to complete our exploration of this beautiful submarine cave. We needed to photograph as much of it as we could. One day, towards the end of the expedition, Martyn and I pulled our way through the bedding just before the end of the outflow, when the water was at its clearest. In these conditions, the visibility was astonishing. With the aid of twin 10-watt Iodin torches, we could look down over 100 ft (30 m) of passage to where things faded into a dusky, distant blue. In Cowrie Haven, the chamber beyond the bedding, we paused and began to take photographs. Any sand we stirred was instantly lost behind us in the outflow, and we swam slowly to Heaven's Gate, rejoicing in the beauty of it all.

This dive rapidly became the most aesthetic of the expedition; the clarity of the water, the rich and varied life, the sheer drama of the situation . . . senses stirred within me, I felt totally at one with my surroundings, utterly at ease in the remote but familiar cave.

With a real sense of loss, I floated to the top of the slope above Heaven's Gate, and looked at the two huge stones for the last time. Then I turned to rejoin Martyn, and the current took us, carrying us back down the long journey to the rising cleft, and thrusting us up into the bright, warm catharsis of the sun.

CHAPTER TWO

Benjamin's early days

T HE EARLIEST of the real Blue Holes explorers was George Benjamin. From the late 1950s, when he first visited Andros, he was captivated by the mysterious cobalt openings in the forests, creeks and reefs of Andros. Born in Latvia, from where he moved to Britain in the 1940s to work as a research chemist, his explorations have only been matched by his professional career as a photographer. In England, he photographed caves in Yorkshire, he climbed and took breathtaking pictures in the Alps, and was one of the first to don SCUBA gear in North America to take pictures in underwater caves.

Having been involved with the development of colour photography as a research scientist for companies such as Agfa, VEF and ICI, George moved to Toronto to establish his own career. There he set up what has now become one of Canada's largest and most successful photographic and processing companies. Somewhere in between all this, he found time to become the leading proponent of Blue Holes exploration in the 1960s and 1970s. Now over seventy years of age, George does not dive for medical reasons, but his memories of years ago are still vivid and clear.

George Benjamin: It was 1968, almost Christmas, and the last diving day of the year. This year I'd been able to spend more time underwater than any other year before. Nonetheless, rough seas had kept me from completing my planned systematic exploration of the deep underwater caves around Mangrove Cay, some 60 miles (96 km) south of my base camp at Stafford Creek, North Andros.

In the dusky half-light before sunrise, Archie Forfar and I loaded my 20 ft (6 m) diveboat, and headed south. The dawn air was cool, and the sea surprisingly calm for the first time in the past month. The tide was still high enough to clear the coral heads that lay scattered in the lagoon, and which had a tendency to appear suddenly in front of the boat in the most unexpected places.

Within two hours we crossed the North Bight, one of the wide saltwater 'rivers' separating the main island that made up the greater jigsaw of Andros itself. The tide was getting low, and we had to make up our minds either to go outside the reef and encounter 5–6 ft (1.5–1.8 m) high waves, or to continue inside, and watch for coral heads. But visibility being good, and the sun now high, we continued inside the lagoon.

We reached Mangrove Cay at noon, an hour after low tide. To approach the cave area, we had to lift our 120 hp stern drive and proceed on a 20 hp auxiliary outboard. Then, for the last few hundred feet, we jumped in the water and pushed the boat over the sands and coral rocks of the real shallows. At the cave mouth we secured two anchors – the Hole was exhausting a whole torrent with tremendous force. From previous experience we knew that the flow would stop three hours after low tide and give us a brief period of calm water before the current turned and began streaming back into the cave.

There was plenty of time to get the equipment ready and test it all. If something did not work today, that would be the end of cave diving for this year – the next useful period for diving in the caves would not be for two weeks. Tomorrow, the calm water would be an hour later, too late for diving and the long ride home the same day. Archie was in a corner of the boat working on diving gear – for safety's sake, he would be wearing twin air tanks with separate regulators. Modern regulators are practically foolproof, but a spare unit could save somebody's life if the other failed. In deeper and more difficult caves, everybody wears two tanks to be absolutely self-contained in case of emergency.

Our lighting equipment was cumbersome, but specially designed for cave exploration. In spite of the above water weight of over 40 lb (18 kg), it was weightless when submerged. Each unit had two bulbs, more powerful than car headlights. The wide-beam flood was intended for general illumination, and the other was a spot beam, so powerful that at night we could illuminate the shoreline, a mile away. But because of the absorption of light by water, this would dim when submerged and, depending on clarity, would penetrate 100 ft (30 m) or less. The diver could choose either bulb. Archie's light was to be mounted next to two powerful strobes, set parallel to the light. In this way, I could aim the direction of my flash and plan my photographs.

My camera was also a cluster of gadgets. A fill-in strobe and small spotlight were attached to the bracket, the latter enabling me to point the camera in the desired direction. A viewfinder was useless in the darkness. During the exploration of big caves, I replaced the small light with a larger one, similar to that of my assistant, enabling me to have everything in one hand with enough light still to explore.

The island of Mangrove Cay lies centrally between the two main parts of Andros. It is only four miles wide, but it is surrounded by at least twenty-three Blue Holes in four distinct areas, so many that we had to identify them by code numbers. This dive was aimed at 'MC21'. MC stood for Mangrove Cay, '21' was the first cave in the second group. We had been diving this cave for years, it was an interesting one, and fairly easy, being 120 ft (36 m) deep at the most. The entrance pit is 20 ft (6 m) wide and 30 ft (9 m) long and, at the bottom, dim daylight is still visible. It contains an impressive passage to the south, 30 ft (9 m) wide and 100 ft (30 m) high, which we had already investigated for at least 200 ft (60 m) without seeing any sign of an end, even with our powerful beams!

The countdown progressed normally. The sky was cloudless, and the temperature pleasant, around 80° F (26° C). An ideal day, quite rare in December. The wind had stopped and the white breakers had disappeared from the reef. The lagoon was like a sheet of glass. I cast my mind back to a day here last April. It was as calm as this, but the doctor-flies and other insects were terrible – only continuous spraying kept them away until after the dive. Insect sprays did not work on a wet body – it seemed the doctor-flies thrived on the taste! They bit even through our neoprene suits. My daughter's light-blue blouse was black with them until, unable to stand it any longer, she put on mask and snorkel, and jumped into the water for relief. But things got worse, and bugs landed in their dozens on her snorkel! After swallowing several, she shot back in the boat, gagging and coughing, and our only escape was to run for the deep water several miles offshore. April is the worst month for bugs; they disappear in July, but then the lagoon is blazing hot. By September, the heat is over, but the autumn storms start to blow. It is rarely possible to win on all counts!

The current was still strong, but the opening was large enough, and we set off. Our first task was to assemble all the equipment on a wide and safe ledge, 30 ft (9 m) down. To counteract the current we used additional weights, which we left at the ledge. Here, we belayed our safety line and lowered a special beacon, which looked rather like a plastic jar with two bulbs inside. It marked the main pit, so that we could regain it from the darkness of the lower cave.

Archie switched on his lights. I retested the camera and strobes, and we descended quickly to the bottom of the pit. The current was hardly noticeable – the main discharge came from the upper passages. We kept at least 10 ft (3 m) from the bottom, in order not to stir up mud. I recalled a dive in the same cave with my Swiss friend, Heinz Bolliger, when he dropped his knife and tried to find it. A moment later I could see only two fins sticking out of a dense cloud of mud. Things suddenly got pitch-black and, as he was carrying the light, I thought the bulb had blown. I tugged him towards me by the firing cord of the strobe, and found that the light was actually still on. Only by pulling along the lifeline were we able to find the surface. His knife is still at the bottom.

Heinz is quite a man, he outweighed us all by many pounds and was such an enthusiastic diver that not only was all the bottom stirred up, but his exhaled bubbles tore loose all the particles from the roof to block visibility completely!

Archie entered the south passage. I followed him, and carefully unwound the safety rope. In those days we used 0.25 in (0.64 cm) nylon, which sank to the bottom and stirred up some mud even with the most careful handling. It was dangerous to use floating rope, such as polyproplene – it got hopelessly entangled in the rugged roofs of the caves, and even in our regulators. A safety man was essential to handle this type of line and, on several occasions, he had to cut brand new ropes to untangle us in time.

Some 200 ft (60 m) inside the passage, Archie switched to spotlight and, as before, the cave appeared to go on forever. I took some photographs, and the flash simply disappeared into blackness, reflecting from nothing. Archie pointed the light towards a formation, and the flash illuminated the whole area as brightly as day. I took over his light to enable him to use both hands to chisel off a fragment for analysis outside. The whole thing did not appear too stable, and I moved some 30 ft (9 m) away. Hanging free in the water, I waited for him to finish.

For the last few minutes, I had experienced some trouble with my mask. It was an old one, but a favourite – it fitted my face so well that I did not like to use anything else. Then, suddenly, it simply disintegrated, leaving me practically blind. For an experienced diver, the loss of a mask does not necessarily constitute a serious situation, even in a cave. I had the lifeline in my hand, but what about Archie? I flickered the light, and the next moment felt him beside me. I showed the OK sign, Archie took the line out of my hand, and then disappeared. As I had the camera still in my hand, I was sure that he had disconnected the firing cable and had surfaced to pick up another mask from the boat.

To my surprise, I felt a pull on the cable. In the darkness, it did not make sense, but Archie suddenly appeared beside me again and pulled me out of the cave. He explained what had happened. He had seen my mask disintegrating and the faceplate dropping to the bottom even before I signalled. He had taken the light out of my hand to try and find it, and reinsert it into my mask. In seconds, the mud was so dense that he could search for it by touch alone. This certainly did not clear up the water! As the light was still attached to my camera, it was no problem for him to find both me and the lifeline again.

I put on another mask and we returned to the bottom of the main shaft. By now, the south passage looked like a volcano, exhausting a dense cloud of mud which slowly drifted up. We retrieved the lifeline and turned our sights on the north passage. There was no current, and the mud stirred up by the lifeline stayed stagnant. We descended the chamber at the end for another 20 ft (6 m), to find it blocked by large boulders. Looking up, we saw a high dome. We ascended almost to the top, but our bubbles stirred fragments from the roof, and these fell to meet us. It was time to get out.

The entrance pit was dark; the clouds of mud from the south passage were following the current, which was still quite strong, out of the cave. We had time for another dive that day, but we now had to look for another cave with clear water!

This was technically easy, as there were at least twenty-three caves around. Nearby was the first group of the Mangrove Cay system, five openings in all, on a straight line, probably part of the same rift zone. Nos 16 and 17 were several hundred feet further east, with enormous currents – especially No. 16! It flowed like an underground river, and the entrance was its broken roof. This pit is 80 ft (24 m) deep, and there are passages in both directions, both of which discharge water into the main entrance pit. Now would be a good time to dive. The diving period here was short, due to the very powerful current, and now it would be almost at a standstill. However, it reached a depth of 160 ft (48 m) inside, and, as nitrogen absorption is cumulative, it would require long decompression.

There were two shallower caves in this system. Nos 12 and 15 were horizontal tunnels, leading in opposite directions from two large daylight funnels. Their depth was only 60 ft (18 m), but the current was considerable. Both were very muddy, and should be entered only during a brisk outflowing current which carries out the stirred-up mud. So they were no good now. In No. 15, we'd found the most beautiful cowrie shells. No. 12 had been entered for at least 300 ft (90 m), and our lights had not picked out any end of a tunnel leading south.

There was a small opening at the far southern end of this group, No. 11, 11,500 ft (3,450 m) from the opening of No. 12. It lay near, or even over, the tunnel of No. 12 but though we suspected a connection between the two, we had so far only found a small pit 30 ft (9 m) deep. The south passage led into a chamber, and the passage in the opposite direction was a fissure, some 2 ft (0.6 m) wide, blocked after 50 ft (15 m).

There were some large mangrove snappers there, though, and we stopped the boat with the intent of shooting a delicious lunch. Archie took the spear and I pointed the light. The spot-lamp appeared to be cracked, apparently broken during my struggles with the mask, but the flood was good and Archie aimed well. We knew that with mangrove snappers we had only one chance – whether we hit or not, the rest would take off. WHAM – we had our dinner, Archie never missed. Fish in hand, we entered the other passage. There was a large king crab at the end – what an appetizer! Archie aimed, but suddenly the crab disappeared into a small opening in the floor, which looked to be very deep. This was exciting!

We surfaced in a hurry, as the current was at a standstill and we did not know how much time we had before the suction commenced. I took my camera and, as one light was blown, two other hand-lamps. We dropped our beacon down after the crab on the end of a 200 ft (60 m) rope. The light looked like a dim glow-worm. We sank down, into an immense pit. One hundred feet down, the walls were already outside the range of our lights, and the beacon at the end *still* looked like a glow-worm! We almost reached it when our second bulb started to fill with water. It was quite remarkable to watch, the light burned till the water reached the filament. Then . . . pfft! As Archie pointed it down, it went out. I fired the strobe, and in the brilliant flash of 32 million candlepower in one 4,000th of a second, I saw the outline of the bottom. We were in little danger, as we still had two hand-torches, and were holding firmly to the guideline. I had no way of knowing the exact direction of the strobe, as the small torch-beam did not reach far. I fired again and again, hoping that my camera was pointing in the right direction at least a few times. I saw the flash image of a great gate, supported by huge pillars, but mostly the light vanished in the immensity of the dome. We slowly ascended the rope, looking up towards the dim outline of the entrance and daylight.

Exploring the entrance to an Andros Blue Hole. *(Photo: Chris Howes FRPS)*

As soon as we entered the cold-water zone, we knew that it was water from the lagoon, and that there would already be some suction at the narrows. At 30 ft (9 m), we stopped. Our decompression meter was well in the red. We had been at 200 ft (60 m) for almost ten minutes which, added to our previous 120 ft (36 m) dive, required about 45 minutes of decompression. For non-divers, it may sound like something horrible, but it simply meant remaining at certain depths for a certain time. In our case, we had to stay at 30 ft (9 m) for 5 minutes, at 20 ft (6 m) for 11 minutes, and at 10 ft (3 m) for 25 minutes. Faster surfacing could cause serious side-effects, the 'bends', which have crippled many divers permanently.

The textbooks advise relaxation during the period. I have tried to be half-asleep, it often works, but not this time. The vivid image of the massive pillars beside the gate was still in my vision. I had the feeling of hanging on a long rope in the middle of an immense dome. Maybe it was only my imagination, or the narcotic effects of nitrogen at great depth? Only the film would show, and only if the camera had been pointing in the right direction.

I relaxed again, there being nothing else to do. I had to decompress for at least the minimum specified time, preferably more. My mind was wandering back some ten years, to when I encountered the Blue Holes of Andros for the first time.

I was exploring the beautiful reef which stretched for 120 miles (192 km) along the east coast of this island. Opposite the north island, the reef forms a solid barrier with only a few openings, but in the south, there are patch reefs of extreme beauty. In some parts, the clarity exceeds 300 ft (90 m), although, within a mile or so this can drop to 20 ft (6 m) or less.

I remember that the ocean was again like polished glass, a dream of a day. I was travelling north in my diveboat, keeping well outside the reef in water at least 50–100 ft (15–30 m) deep. The water was so exceptionally clear that I could see the shadows of the coral heads that the sun cast on the white sandy bottom. I got dizzy – this was not like boating on water, but like flying. I looked over the side of the boat – the coral gardens seemed suspended in air and I could clearly see the drop-off at 150 ft (44 m), where the deep reef vanished into the abyss many thousand feet deep, over the natural phenomena we called the 'Wall'.

After a successful day of diving and exploring, I was looking for shelter. The village at the end of the deep bay was accessible only at a relatively high tide and, a few hundred yards from the shore, I was caught solidly by the outgoing sea. Well, I figured that tomorrow the tide would be high again, and I was in great need of a good rest.

This was one of the many friendly villages where a white visitor was a rarity. I knew some of the natives from previous visits; their accommodation was primitive, but spotlessly clean and, for sure, more comfortable than my boat. Wading ashore, I soon found a bed for the night. The lady of the house, to my delight, was an excellent cook of native food. Freshly caught crawfish – Bahamian lobster – were steamed in seaweed and seasoned with spices and peppers and limes from the backyard.

I retired soon after dinner. Almost asleep, I heard peculiar noises, beating drums, and distant singing. At first I thought I was dreaming, but when the noise grew louder, I looked through the window and almost fainted. A procession was moving towards the house, chanting and pounding drums. I swear that in the moonlight I saw long spears being carried by those in front, and other tools of torture by those behind, and I heard the roll of large kettles, most certainly used to boil missionaries! The situation appeared hopeless – I was the only white man for many miles, my boat was solidly aground, and there was nowhere to hide.

My landlady assured me that this was a regular Saturday night church parade. She ought to know, she said, as her father was a preacher and headed the procession. For me, it looked and sounded like an ancient sacrificial ceremony. I had the feeling that my delicious dinner had only been stuffing for the feast to come.

Some of the men, at that moment the nastiest-looking ones, split from the procession and headed straight for my lodging. I felt as if I had been caught bare-handed in the middle of a school of hungry sharks. Fortunately, everything turned out well. The men were relatives looking for beer, and the parade was real. I never found out whether it had been coincidence, or specially staged to honour – or horrify – me. The men were quite different than I had imagined them a short while ago, and as I could help them out with beer from my boat, they became very talkative.

Each bottle consumed made their stories more hair-raising. I was still shivering, and of course did not tell them the reason why, so they related it to their wild stories. They had heard of my diving activities before, but said that, for goodness sake, I should keep away from the Blue Holes. They were peopled by monstrous octopuses, sometimes called 'Lusca'! These creatures would shoot their tentacles out of the water and, if one should grip you, you were dead, my boy! There were many skeletons in the Blue Holes. The 'Chickcharnies', birdlike monsters in the forests, could put a curse on you, and you would be dizzy and go round in circles for the rest of your life. There was a bottomless Blue Hole right here in the swampy backyard and, when I expressed a wish to dive, I was treated with pity. The beer was finished, and the stories broke off most abruptly.

Next morning, some of the bravest villagers escorted me to the Blue Hole. My landlady was dressed in black, and politely enquired how to dispose of my belongings. We did find the Blue Hole, but it was not quite as bottomless as recounted last night. I could see the bottom at 15 ft (4.5 m) and, before I stirred up mud, the visibility was good. I did not find anything. No octopuses shot their tentacles at me, but it was my first dive in a real Andros Blue Hole.

Some time later, I flew on the local airline to Nassau. It was low tide, and a clear day. I saw many more dark spots than before, because I now knew what to look for. Usually, shallow holes appear a light green colour, and only the deep ones look dark. From the left window I clearly saw the great Blue Hole of Conch Sound, with its multiple openings. On the other side, I saw a large blue circle. It appeared quite bottomless. Later, I explored it with my boat and, when my sonar only showed it to be 25 ft (7.5 m) deep, I nearly threw the expensive instrument overboard. I dove down the vertical wall. The sonar was correct, there was the bottom, despite its dark-blue colour.

On the other hand, in the middle of the North Bight, there is a distinct dark circle some 300 ft (90 m) across. The locals claim their lines are too short to reach the bottom, and that gigantic sharks tear them into shreads. Once again I did not believe my sonar, the signals simply disappeared. I let down over 230 ft (70 m) of fishing line. After the shark stories, it took me a long time to get up enough courage to dive. As the visibility was less than 20 ft (6 m), the atmosphere was horrifying. At 50 ft (15 m), the slope dropped off into a vertical pit. There was a thermocline, the water temperature dropped several degrees and somehow the visibility doubled. At 150 ft (45 m), we hit another zone of murky water and, within 10 ft (3 m), the visibility dropped again, to less than before. We never saw the bottom and also, to my considerable relief, no sharks or other creatures.

My interest in Blue Holes grew, and I engaged some of the best local guides. The first was Ivan Johnson from Fresh Creek. At that time, he was the only Androsian with any experience in SCUBA, and he showed me some deep scars on his legs and proudly declared them shark bites. To me, they resembled cuts from a propeller or some such machinery but, as I depended on his services, I expressed no doubts; he was a good diver and knew the reef well. He also knew of a small cave 5 miles (8 km) to the south, one of the first Blue Holes ever explored. A party lead by Betty Singer had, several years before, descended to 100 ft (30 m) with only small handlamps. The entrance fell 40 ft (12 m) to a passage leading north to a chamber, at a depth of 120 ft (36 m). The bottom was incredibly muddy.

In those days, I was diving with my friends Tom and Carol McCollum and Jack Birch. We had our first ever underwater film light ready, and I was planning to film a silhouette sequence of Tom carrying it down. Jack was our safety man, and went down first wearing his black leotards. I followed, and took up position in the passage at 40 ft (12 m), wedging myself in between the walls to get a solid support. I could hardly see Jack in his black leotards a few feet below. During the scene, I slowly sank to the bottom and accidentially touched him. His leotards seemed rather rough. Tom looked horrified, and only by his lights did I see that it was not Jack, but a soundly sleeping 7 ft (2 m) nurse shark. Jack was deeper in the passage waiting for us.

Ivan was an honest man, if only in that he did not claim to know any more Blue Holes. He advised us to see his uncle 'Captain' Joe Johnson. I met him at Staniard Creek, one of the romantic villages, and Captain Joe appeared to be an authority on everything. He showed us a small but interesting cave near Rat Cay, which had all the features of big caves, but everything was in miniature. The opening was only 20 ft (6 m) deep, and to the south there was a low passage, split by many pillars. There were many species of fish, and we occasionally saw a monstrous Horse-eye Jack. It was 5 ft (1.5 m) long, and must have weighed over 100 lb (45 kg).

The westward tunnel led to a narrow fissure leading to the lower cave, at 40 ft (12 m). It was a wide, low passage, which for us ended 150 ft (45 m) in, fizzling out in cracks too small for us to penetrate. The clarity at this cave was superb.

After this episode, we went south. During the long trip I started to wonder about 'Captain' Johnson's title. Bahamian titles are somewhat unclear to me. There are many dukes, knights, counts, even a king, but they are all actually musicians. For sure, he did not appear to have captained the *Queen Mary*, if his operation of my boat was any clue. We did not hit many rocks, as it was high tide. We smashed only one propeller and when I put on the spare I played safe, and took the wheel myself. At Mangrove Cay, he contacted some of his friends. The language is English, I am told, but to me it sounded like Chinese. The verdict was that there were no Blue Holes there – all of them were in the north – so we headed home. Only later did I discover that we were then only a few hundred yards from the densest cave area of all. Our guide deserved an admiral's title for leading us through this area without hitting at least some of them by sheer chance alone.

It took several years to discover this, until one day I flew home from Jamaica during the Cuban blockade. The plane was rerouted over South Andros, and I could hardly believe my eyes – the area was littered with Blue Holes!

CHAPTER THREE

South Bight and the Wall

W HERE ANDROS got its name from, no one really knows. It was once thought to be Greek, Andros being settled in the last century by Greek fishermen who soon made this new island as famous for sponges as their old home, the Mediterranean Andros. But the name was found on maps long before the Greek influx.

A seventeenth-century story relates the island to the British Colonial Governor of New England, Sir Edmund Andros, who received, as a grant from the British Crown, an island in the Bahamas. Details are obscure, and it is also possible that the island was confused with San Andreas, an island off the central American coast. Just by coincidence, San Andreas is located at the same distance and direction from the notorious seventeenth-century pirate stronghold of Providence Island as our Andros is from Nassau, on New Providence – which, by chance, happened to be another popular pirate watering hole.

Andros today is an island of contrasts. New roads have been built, and regular airlines connect Andros with Nassau and the US mainland. In villages as peaceful as the South Pacific, there are homes which have fast American cars in the driveway and satellite discs for colour televisions. There are clean houses hidden in banana groves with well-tended flower gardens, but there are also scruffy shacks, surrounded by garbage and such junk as broken beds, old refrigerators, and dead and dying cars, which after a while one is inclined to consider as regular front-lawn furniture. Poverty does not necessarily equate with lack of cleanliness, and some of the poorest Androsians are the most houseproud. There are old fishermen, still working from traditional Bahamian sloops and small rowing boats, blowing conch shells to announce their catch to the world, alongside islanders who race around at full throttle in fibreglass outboards.

The Bahamians, and especially the Androsians, have been boatbuilders for centuries. There are still great craftsmen among them, even if their techniques are slightly primitive, beginning first with a search through the woods for trees of the right shape, which they trim into ready-bent ribs. Bahamians rarely hurry; it could take years, maybe decades, to finish one of their famous sloops. Calculating a minimum wage, the price would be, by modern standards, prohibitive. A craft was the pride of the community and its seaworthiness was astonishing. A 24–30 ft (7–9 m) sloop would be capable of carrying twenty or more passengers, plus tons of fish, and crossing open sea for hundreds of miles. Sadly, the boatbuilding industry is in decline, for modern mail-boats and custom-built craft are an easier alternative for ocean travel.

Dr George Benjamin and son George Junior during the Blue Hole dives of the early 1970s. *(Photo: Benjamin collection)*

Andros is the largest Bahamian island, about 100 miles (160 km) long and up to 40 miles (64 km) wide. Its low surface is cut into a fragmented jigsaw by saltwater creeks, rivers and deep bays. At high tide, the island shrinks considerably, but even then its total mass is as much as all the other Bahamian islands put together. To the east, the deep abyss of the 'Tongue of the Ocean' falls from the edge of the reef to over 6,000 ft (1,800 m), separating Andros from New Providence and the long scattered chain of the Exuma Cays. On all other sides, the island is surrounded by the shallow Great Bahama Bank, a marine plateau as shallow as the island is high. Approach by sea was notoriously difficult, many ships foundered on the fringing barrier reef (one of the world's longest) and the island became a safe refuge for runaway slaves early in modern Bahamian history. Even now, the Androsians live almost entirely on the east coast, and at about 8,000, form only 5 per cent of the total population of the Bahamas.

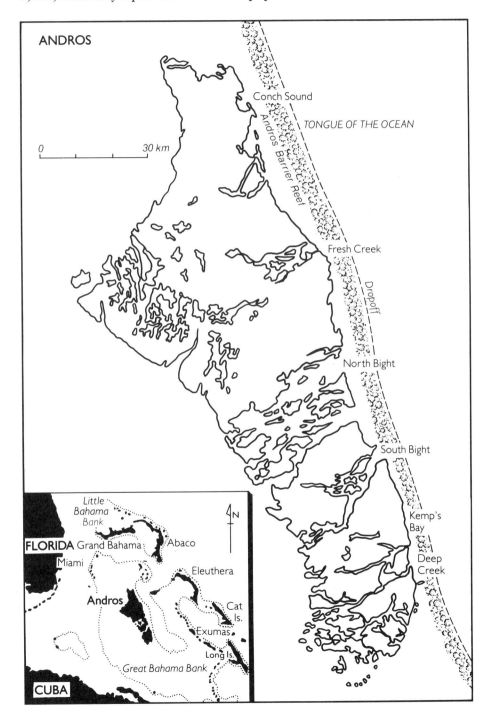

Economically, Andros depends on imports. Local fishing is still profitable, though stocks of crawfish, conch and reef fish have steadily declined over the past decades as fishing methods have improved, changing from the old handline and glass-bottomed bucket to nylon nets and outboard motors. Agriculture is mininal; save for an experimental, government-run farm on the North Island, most crops are grown for subsistence alone, and farming is really still in the slash-and-burn stage. Small patches of forest are chopped, farmed for a year or two until what soil there is in the crevices and banana holes is exhausted, then left to regenerate into an even thicker, more tangled scrub than before.

Forestry has been important, and may yet be again. The northern pinewoods have twice been completely logged to provide pit-props for British mines and pulp for Chicago newspapers, clearing several indigenous species in the process – perhaps also seeing off the last 'Chickcharnies', the giant owls that formed the basis for legends of red-eyed, three-toed elves that lived in caves and trees and brought ill-luck to whoever tampered with them. Most of the exotic hardwoods, mahogany and lignum vitae, the 'tree of life', went long ago.

So did the sponges, the brightly coloured marine animals that made Andros famous in the last century. In 1935 the sponge-beds were wiped out by disease and, though the beds are now returning, artificial alternatives mean natural sponges are no longer competitive.

Tourism has not yet caught on, with the exception of the old diving resort, the most famous (and longest lasting) being Small Hope Bay, run by George Benjamin's old companion, Dick Birch. The highlight of a stay at Small Hope is diving the 'Wall'!

George Benjamin: As a side project, we explored the incredible underwater cliff off the eastern side of Andros that we simply called the 'Wall'. We did not intend to look for the deepest caves of all – perhaps thousands of feet down the slopes – but felt, for obvious reasons, that it was more promising to examine the Wall at the ancient ocean lows of the Ice Ages, 200–300 ft (60–90 m) below today's level.

We made many hundreds of dives in the 1950s and 1960s – in 1968 alone I listed 87 dives over 230 ft (70 m). We searched the Wall from the Berry Islands to the southern tip of Andros, but found no long, open caves. There were, however, numerous shallow caves, ledges and overhangs, all of which could be the remains of old cavern entrances.

On the other hand, those deep dives were experiences in themselves. Even though Wall dives became almost routine, they were still thrilling, and the scenery tremendously colourful, especially through the eyes of a photographer. It always came as a surprise that, as we played our lights on them, the colour of sponges, gorgonians and algae at such depths seemed so much more vivid than those nearer the surface.

Several diving records using ordinary compressed air have been set here.

In 1961, Betty Singer set a world record for women, her 310 ft (93 m) dive being supervised by a young Canadian doctor, Joe McInnis, now one of the great authorities on diving in Canada, and an accomplished medic and film maker. Then, in 1962, Dick Birch and Roger Hutchins went down to 462 ft (139 m). I don't know what this proved, but in any case, it was a world record.

A Wall dive has three distinct parts. It starts with the descent to the top of the Wall, which is usually 150–170 ft (45–50 m). Often the top 30–50 ft (9–15 m) are murky, and the anchor rope appears to vanish into nothing. To dive away from the sight of the surface is an awesome feeling. As soon as I lost the reference point of the boat and before I could spot the bottom, I got the same dizzy sensation as I would looking over a high mountain cliff.

Going over the edge of the Wall is like flying a small plane into the Grand Canyon – and the descent is like falling slowly down a huge mountain face. As we were weightless, there was no feeling of vertigo, even looking straight down for many hundred feet. Occasionally there are thermoclines, notably at 200–220 ft (60–66 m), where the water temperatures may fall by as much as 5° F, with an increase in clarity to several hundred feet. By this depth, the effects of pressure and nitrogen narcosis have begun to appear. There are great individual differences, and novices suffer more. I feel an absolute, timeless silence, which I cannot easily describe and which is, for me, unique. I fully understand Cousteau's choice of title for *The Silent World*.

I made many Wall dives with Douglas Faulkner, a successful underwater photographer from the USA. I have never met anyone as keen on Wall diving as he was. Despite his experience, he readily admitted to nitrogen narcosis. As photography was his living, he secured his camera settings with tape, as he simply could not remember the proper setting on deep dives. We were once at 240 ft (72 m), looking at George Junior, my son, going down to a tremendous red gorgonian which was at least 50 ft (15 m) below. George went down 10 ft (3 m), looked at his depth gauge, went another 10 ft (3 m), looked again, and so on. He tried to focus his camera from 10 ft (3 m) away. This seemed strange, as we knew he was using a close-up device. I shot down and pulled him up. The next moment, he shot back down like a loaded spring to close-up distance and fired. After the dive, he explained that at that moment he was sure that he was at 245 ft (73.5 m), as under the influence of narcosis he was unable to figure out that that was the limit of the depth gauge, and that it would read no further. He was also unable to work out why the camera did not focus. George was 20 years old at the time, with six years' experience of Wall diving, and he knew what nitrogen narcosis was about. My good friend Heinz Bolliger claimed that he was never affected. During one of our 270 ft (80 m) dives, I shot a whole roll of thirty photographs at him. I almost lost his friendship when he saw what really happened.

We were able to remain at this depth for only a few minutes. During the ascent narcosis disappears and sounds come back at the edge of the drop-off. George reports a strange feeling, as if coming out of a dream, as a fulfilment, of something gigantic. The few minutes down seem to be almost endless. He compares a Wall dive with the effects of LSD. I suspect he has not told me everything.

The slow return to the surface leads to the final step, decompression, and that can take a long time, especially after repeated dives. Many years of diving proved to me that treating the tables very conservatively paid good dividends, as I never suffered serious after-effects.

Naturally, like any explorer, I have been asked what I intended to find, and whether it made any sense to take unavoidable risks and enter underwater caves at all. I did not expect to find hidden pirate's gold, in brass-bound boxes. Even if I had, that would not be the main reason. I have been exploring caves all my life. It's more the feeling of adventure, the great feeling of putting your foot where no other has been before. I have crawled through low passages half in water and mud for miles, descended rope-ladders to my last bit of strength to break through barriers and suddenly enter a magnificent dome or pit, ornamented with the most beautiful stalactites, sometimes pure white, sometimes in the most unusual colours. A cave above water counts as being explored when an impassable barrier of rock or mud is reached, or the roof lowers into a pool. This is where our exploration of underwater caves only begins.

Mountaineers have an advantage; they know their target. In most cases, it is visible before their eyes, and in times of difficulty, this can give additional strength. Cave explorers have no such visible goal, but have always the chance to find something deeper, greater or more beautiful – the un-expected!

Our discovery of the great pit in MC11 might have been the result of a great deal of luck. But it was by no means a wild goose chase. By systematic research we knew it had to be there, where great pits were to be expected. Sooner or later, we would have hit it. It had been the coincidence of our bad luck in cave No. 21 which gave us the additional time, and the escape of the red crab into the unseen fissure. Maybe the next time the spear would have missed the fish, and dropped down into the fissure. Being in the right place at the right time is what counts. Knowing where the right place is, helps.

Look, for example, at the discovery of the longest cave system in the English Pennines, 'Easegill Caverns'. The study of local geology suggested that great caves were to be found, and the area was searched for years. One day, a group of potholers were sitting down after a long and unsuccessful hunt. Although it was winter, one of the men felt warm air coming out of the ground (the apocryphal story has it he had crept behind some bushes to squat and relieve himself – if so, it must have come as a pleasant surprise). After shifting some stones, they uncovered a small hole. At first only small men could enter, but it was widened to reveal it as one of the first entrances to a system which is today over 40 miles (64 km) long and over 500 ft (150 m) deep.

Back in Toronto, in my photographic laboratories, I developed the film from MC11, to see whether it had been nitrogen narcosis, or reality. I secured the film in the tank as carefully as I had secured the lifeline at the top of the pit. The room was as dark as the cave, and the illuminated dials looked like the beacon in the deep shaft. It was time to turn on the light. There were many blank frames where I had missed the flash completely; there were many shots with clear and brilliant images of the immense dome, and there, in one corner – the 'gate' and the 'columns'. It looked quite different from the flash images, but it was there, it was real, it was great!

Rob Palmer: It might help to understand why there are so many Blue Holes in the Bahamas – and, of course, just what a Blue Hole is.

The Bahama Banks sit on top of the greatest known mass of limestone in the world, over 5 vertical miles (8 km) of accumulated marine sediments that lie in almost perfectly horizontal layers, or 'beds'. No mountain building has ever taken place here, only a slow, almost imperceptible subsidence as new layers of limestone rocks are laid down, and the pressure forces the rock below even deeper into the Earth. This happens far too slowly for any single generation to be aware of – in the last 8,000 years, far longer than man has settled the islands, they have sunk only by a single foot. Five miles (8 km) of rock represents aeons – the Bahamas began forming at the same time as the Atlantic Ocean, when the great super-continent of Panagea split apart over 150,000,000 years ago.

Waving gorgonians and massive brain corals fringe one of the many marine Blue Holes off South Andros. *(Photo: Chris Howes FRPS)*

For most of this immense time, the Bahamas have been simply low atolls, coral reefs fringing an inner lagoon of soft sands and muds, formed when the soupy lagoon water evaporated and dumped its load of calcium carbonate – embryonic limestone – on the floor of the sea. Tidal movements rolled the minute limestone fragments around, gathering them into larger balls, or 'oolites'. The sheer weight of new oolites forming on old helped cement the balls together into a simple form of limestone, friable, and easily broken by other forces. At the same time, countless billions of tiny marine organisms were living and dying out on the surrounding reef, and their skeletal remains (also calcium carbonate) gathered and grew on their foundation of even more ancient reefs into deep supporting layers around the inner lagoon. This harder limestone formed a sort of wall around the softer, inner material, effectively holding the Bahama Banks together as they grew.

The Bahamas lie at the edge of the *continental plate* of North America, the great floating 'island' of rock that sits on top of the molten magma far below. The American land plate is still slowly pulling away from Europe and Asia, stretching the floor of the Atlantic Ocean slowly wider. This might be partly responsible for the creation of the deep marine trenches of the 'Tongue of the Ocean' and 'Exuma Sound', where the Banks have been separated by troughs many thousands of feet deep, the bottoms of which now lie far below the levels at which the limestone grew. The great faults which orginally formed these may also have helped form the caves – the giant fracture that runs down the eastern coast of Andros, on which many of the main Blue Holes lie, may be where the edge of the Bank is slowly falling into the 'Tongue', or it may simply be the surface of a massive fracture that extends many thousands of feet down to the very foundations of the Bahamas, along the edge of the American plate. It is possible to align many of the inland and ocean Blue Holes along this fracture, and other such fractures that lie parallel, or at particular angles, to it.

George believed that the caves themselves had been formed by the action of great underwater rivers. These, he thought, flowed below the islands during the much lower sea-levels that existed during the most recent Ice Ages, when much of the water in the world's oceans was frozen into the great ice-sheets that extended out from the Poles. In this he was partly right; the low seas were definitely responsible for the levels at which many of the caves formed, and water movements through the caves certainly would have enlarged them. But it seems that the caves were there before sea-level fell far. As soon as the islands began to emerge, rainwater started gathering below them in the porous, fissured rock. Instead of simply mixing immediately with the underlying saltwater, great freshwater 'lenses' formed. These were shallower towards the edge of the island, or near creeks, but could have reached thicknesses of several hundred feet in the middle of the Banks at the height of the Ice Age.

Where freshwater and saltwater met, a peculiar chemical magic took place. Though both types of water were already saturated with dissolved minerals, where they met and mingled they formed a third type, a brackish mix that was now very 'aggressive', and which could dissolve the surrounding rock more quickly than either the fresh or saline layers. Tidal flow running through the fissured rock along the base of the lens removed this water, and slowly formed cave passages along the network of fissures. Particular sea-levels were responsible for the levels of the caves – where the seas stood long enough in one place, caves formed. When they rose or fell, the level of cave formation rose or fell in response, removing the walls of fissures like an immense natural plane, or dissolving horizontal beds of rock that were weaker than those above or below. This somewhat selective process went on for tens if not hundreds of thousands of years. This meant that some of the caves are very big indeed!

The oldest caves, those which formed before the seas fell far, were, for part of their existence at least, above water. While the seas were down, beautiful galleries of stalactites and stalagmites formed in the now-dry passages. Dripstones such as these cannot form underwater, and even if the caves were dry, surface conditions would have to be right – lots of rain to create lots of drips.

George had a particular dream. He wanted to discover stalagmites and stalactites deep underwater in his beloved Blue Holes. He was certain that they must be there. But though he had explored such caves for over ten years, there had been no sight of the crystal forms. Then came the discovery of one of the most dramatic systems of all, beneath the South Bight of Andros.

George Benjamin: We had been diving in the South Bight since 1966, and had looked inside over ten openings that lay in three parallel lines across the mouth of the Bight. Some of these were too small to enter, simply cracks that ebbed and flowed with the changing cave tides. Here, as at Mangrove Cay, we catalogued the caves by numbers. Most of our attention had been paid to No. 2, where a spectacular pit fell vertically to 110 ft (33 m). In midsummer, an incredibly beautiful view could be gained by dropping to the base of the pit and watching divers silhouetted by the overhead sun as they descended. The current was light and diving was possible at any time, though the superb clarity lasted for only a short while, when low tide coincided with the maximum outflow. It was remarkable – during this period the lagoon above was hot and murky and looking from the boat, the cave was hardly visible. As soon as the entrance was reached, the view opened up tremendously. On the other hand, during inflow, the lagoon was reasonably clear, but the visibility in the cave was appalling!

At the bottom of the pit were two passages leading in opposite directions. The south passage was muddy, and could be entered at low tide, even when the current was at maximum outflow. There was a high dome 150 ft (45 m) inside, where the ceiling rose out of the range of our lights. Our exhaled bubbles, wobbling upwards, detached white, flaky silt from the roof, and these descended slowly, like snowflakes. So inevitably we called this the 'Snowflake Room'. The main passage went on beyond, at this 140 ft (42 m) level.

The north passage was less muddy, and a much stronger current was encountered. It could be entered either at high 'standstill', when the cave flow paused some 3½ hours after high tide, or at low standstill, some 4–5 hours later. The cave tides were out of phase with those on the surface, for reasons we then did not fully understand, but it was essential that we charted them accurately to ensure we knew exactly when it was safe to enter. This passage was remarkable – the low standstill was unusually long, and entry could be made over a period of an hour or more. The corresponding period in surrounding caves was much shorter, sometimes only five minutes before the tidal flow reversed and picked up speed. The passage was entered for 300 ft (90 m) to a massive rockfall which blocked further progress. Two hundred feet (60 m) in, there was a high room, a counterpart to the 'Snowflake Room', though this one was comparatively clean.

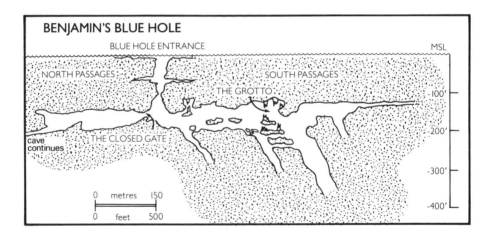

The exploration of the great Blue Hole, SB4, was one of the most exciting periods of my Blue Hole career. The first descent of the great entrance pit had been at Christmas 1967, and as soon as we entered this cave, we realized that it was much larger than anything we had seen before. We proceeded cautiously, step by step. Sixty feet (18 m) down, the sloping shaft gave way to a vertical chasm. The view down below was horrifying – the cave disappeared into an immense void, beyond the range of our spotlights. We belayed the vital lifeline and proceeded downwards. It took three nerve-racking attempts to reach the bottom, at 210 ft (63 m). There, the cave had only just begun.

In the summer of 1970, Captain Jacques Cousteau came to Andros in his *Calypso*, to make a TV special on the Blue Holes. The highlight of this film was to be the discovery of stalagmites and stalactites in the Andros caves, like those filmed already in the great Blue Hole of Lighthouse Reef in Belize, an enormous circular hole in the middle of the sea-floor. They had used mini-submarines to get over 400 ft (120 m) down in the pit, nearly losing Falco, their chief diver, in the process, when his submarine became trapped on a ledge. Now they wanted to add the Bahamian caves to their shotlist, but had spent several weeks searching for the elusive formations without success.

I took Cousteau's team into every cave I could imagine. We found many features that looked like stalactites, but none had crystalline cores, all were simply rock pillars. Disappointed, Cousteau and *Calypso* left, but I was determined to go deeper and further into the caves in the hope of finding these elusive crystal stones.

By this time, we had reached the limit of our technical ability, and had only explored an area of 300 ft (90 m) around the base of the main pit. Before further exploration was possible, we had to adapt our equipment and methods for deeper penetration. The breathing apparatus and auxiliary systems could have no flaws. The same applied to the lighting. The size and weight of all equipment including cameras and strobe-lights had to be kept to a minimum to lessen drag. Plastic reels were designed to eliminate the bulky coils of hand-held safety rope. By tabulating the tides and the time lags, we predicted the currents and extended our safe diving time. We could not chance being trapped in the cave by a whirlpool.

By late 1970 we had explored the passages for several hundred feet to north and south. The North Passage had seemed to be blocked by rockfall 100 ft (30 m) in, the 'Closed Gate', but a narrow fissure high in the cave led into a continuation, which we later followed for almost 2,000 ft (600 m) without finding the end. For obvious reasons, we entered the large openings first!

By September, with the help of Tom Mount and Dick Williams, two expert cave divers from Miami, we had penetrated 1,000 ft (300 m) inside the cave to the south, at a maximum depth of 260 ft (78 m). Some of the pits we swam over were so deep that we could not see the bottom. The cave was so gigantic that in our search we had to neglect the numerous smaller openings, one of them high inside the South Passage. When we did find time to examine this, we discovered two pillars, 3 ft (0.9 m) tall, which looked suspiciously like cave stalagmites. Were they genuine, or simply residues from beach rock or pillar coral? We had been disappointed so many times before. Naturally, we could not think of breaking them off to find out; we would have to return with a core drill. But then, looking back, we saw high in the roof a solid column formed by a stalactite joining a stalagmite. It was, beyond doubt, a real dripstone. This small opening also proved to be the key to the rest of the cave.

One of Benjamin's team approaches the 'Closed Gate' in the North Passage of Benjamin's Blue Hole. High in the roof above this, the way on leads over 2,000 ft (600 m) of new cave passages. *(Photo: Dr George Benjamin)*

Eight hundred feet (240 m) inside this passage, we came to a huge room. A fallen slab was wedged between the walls, forming a natural bridge. The passage was littered with breakdown slabs. We were at the end of our lifeline, and had to stop. The clarity was superb, ideal for pictures, so I held on to the very end of the lifeline while Dick went 50 ft (15 m) ahead of me, using the firing cord that extended from my camera to the strobe as an extension of the guideline. Tom was yet another 20 ft (6 m) ahead. This was our standard photographic set-up – the diver in front of the strobe indicated the proper scale for the picture.

Within the reach of Tom's light, I saw the faint outline of a cavern filled with stalactites and stalagmites. I switched off my own lights to view the spectacular scene from total darkness. Then I lit the cavern up by firing the strobe. By the light of the brilliant flashes I could see that this was only the beginning of a vast network of formations. Our time was running out. Minutes had passed quickly. We had to hurry back.

The brief glimpses of the Grotto opened up an entirely new chapter in underwater caving. I contacted Cousteau, and he found it unbelievable. In November, with the help of Frank Martz, an underwater engineer from Tampa and an experienced Florida cave diver, we worked our way into the South Passage and laid a permanent guideline into the Boulder Room and the natural bridge. This was our stopping point in September. This time we were better equipped, and we pushed on. Fifty feet (15 m) further, we were among the stalagmites, and we entered a maze of passages in between cave formations, some of them 10 ft (3 m) tall. We did not know the geography of the cavern, and had to be careful not to lose the way as we stirred up fine silt from the bottom, and our exhaled bubbles detached flakes from the ceiling. Frank carried the reel, and I shone the light. After a few dives, we became familiar with the layout of the Grotto. There were two distinct galleries. The lower one started just beyond the rock bridge, at a depth of 150–190 ft (45–57 m), while the upper part started at 150 ft (45 m), with a cluster of stalagmites which we named the 'Roman Bridge'. This ascended to a crystal cascade at 90 ft (27 m).

The passage continued beyond the Grotto, and the floor fell away into a gigantic pit. Frank was fascinated by this, and we descended to 260 ft (78 m) without seeing the bottom. I had to stop him here; it was beyond my limits to go further, but he intended to return and go deeper as soon as the chance arose. A high-level passage continued above the pit, and Tom Mount and Ike Ikehara entered this for 600 ft (180 m) without finding the end, gaining a point over 2,000 ft (600 m) from the cave entrance.

Phillipe Cousteau was most enthusiastic about our discovery, and we met again on Andros late in the year. Our new experience and refined equipment now provided the necessary safety cover for the divers from *Calypso*. Jacques Cousteau flew in himself for the filming dives, and he and his divers used underwater flares to illuminate the cavern. I watched from the same position where, only a few months ago, I had held the end of the lifeline and seen the Grotto for the first time. Then there was only a faint light. Now there was a galaxy of burning flares. It was three years to the day since Peter and I had discovered the great Blue Hole and entered the pit.

After the discovery of SB4, it was natural to spend all our time there. This was our greatest discovery of all. By the end of 1970, we had laid over 1.25 miles (2 km) of permanent guidelines into the maze of passages. The main passage was explored to north and south for a combined total of 4,000 ft

(1,200 m). The South Passage was longest, just over 2,000 ft (600 m), the North Passage being just a little less. It was evident by comparing measurements taken on the surface that we had by-passed the other openings in the middle of the Bight by several hundred feet. Our survey techniques were not quite accurate enough to determine exactly how far apart the South Passage of SB4 and the North Passage of SB2 were – they could have been very close, or they could have been a hundred feet or more.

It seemed likely that the caves would connect, and could be regarded as one system. By the connection of such associated cave systems, the longest caves in the world have been explored. Underwater connections had been made between springs in nearby Florida and, though these were more similar to caves on dry land, there seemed no reason not to expect such a connection between the South Bight Holes. Our theory was strengthened by evaluating aerial photographs and making underwater measurements. It appeared that the openings of SB1, 2 and 3, and an adjacent chain of dark patches, were almost overhead of the South Passage in No. 4. We attempted to interconnect these entrances.

So, in July 1971, we by-passed the rockfall in the North Passage of SB2. The lower passage was blocked, but by coming back some 20 ft (6 m), a chimney led over the top of the blockage and into the continuation of the cave. To our delight, there were some stalagmites. At 400 ft (120 m) the passage split, and we explored the left branch for the same distance again, slowly descending to a depth of 160 ft (48 m). There was a strong current, and we swam cautiously.

On our next dive we took the right fork, and within just 20 ft (6 m) came across a forest of candle-like stalagmites. It is inconceivable how poor underwater observation can be. Four years ago we simply did not see the obvious continuation of the passage. On our last dive we did not see a multitude of formations, right in front of our noses.

This grotto was in a tunnel some 10 sq ft. The candle-like stalagmites stretched almost to the ceiling and, after wriggling through the openings between the formations, the bottom dropped 10 ft (3 m) to a cluster of pillars 20 ft (6 m) high. The material was heavily eroded, both by re-solution and by little marine organisms boring into the rock, but one small sample we took out showed a distinctive crystal core. The stalagmites continued for another 50 ft (15 m), and a total of 800 ft (240 m) was explored in strong currents without finding any end.

Openings 1 and 3 were explored without much success; the most we could do was get 100 ft (30 m) inside, to a depth of 80 ft (24 m). The passages were too tight for our twin tanks to get through. The only possibility would have been to take the tanks off and push them in front – not something any of us relished much. Both of these entrances lie above the passages of SB2 but, though we discharged several tanks of compressed air in likely places below, and released dye, neither was observed in the creek above.

During these tests we made another unexpected discovery. When releasing air in the Snowflake Room, the amount of material that came down was incredible. Despite this, we decided to ascend. It was a strange feeling, going up and up, knowing that there would be no air surface above. At 40 ft (12 m), we came to the roof. There were massive stalactites, 10 ft (3 m) long, the shallowest find so far. The walls were covered with crystal 'organ pipes', and a sound lifeline was essential for a safe return. The unusually shallow stalactites ended abruptly at 60 ft (18 m). Why? Maybe there was a lake on the floor of the dome at the time. Perhaps this is why there are also no corresponding stalagmites?

Our efforts to connect the caves met with no success. And the summer ended in tragedy.

Rob Palmer: By the end of August 1971 George Benjamin and his friends had made many mapping and exploration dives in the new caverns beneath Sough Bight with absolute safety. They had decided early on that they had limitations – the caves were extremely deep, their greatest depths being far beyond what is safe if breathing ordinary compressed air. To go further safely would require special breathing mixes of helium and oxygen, and such greater depths, they decided, were beyond their accepted safety limits – limits which had kept them alive without real incident for years.

The Florida cave divers who were working with them, headed by Tom Mount, had laid guidelines to a depth of 300 ft (90 m) in the pit beyond the Grotto in SB4, now renamed by Cousteau 'Benjamin's Blue Hole'. To allow for safer, long-distance penetrations, George had designed the 'Benjamin Crossover', a manifold that connected two back-mounted air tanks together, and allowed two breathing regulators to be worn. A unique valve system allowed each regulator to have access to the air in both tanks, but if one regulator failed, it could be isolated without compromising the other system. This improved diving safety considerably – till then, many of the Florida cave divers had simply been using a small extra tank with an extra regulator attached to their main tank.

The added impetus of the Florida divers pushed the limits of the caves further and further back – towards the very limits of safety. This was of some concern to George. One of his prime considerations was the safety of all those involved with his work and he was slightly unhappy to concede that, to push the frontiers of the caves back, he must accept standards that were new to him. He had the highest regard for the bravery of the Florida divers, and they certainly provided the push that took him beyond his previous limits of discovery.

Much was being achieved, and generally things were going pretty smoothly. On the 26th, Tom made an inventory of all the diving equipment on board, which read like the contents of a dive shop, and preparations began for the next series of dives.

On the following day, as Benjamin and his team were preparing to enter the water, another boat pulled up. On it were Jim Lockwood, an experienced Florida cave diver, and John Carcelle, a virtual novice. They wanted to dive in the cave, and there was little that Benjamin could do to dissuade them. George had met Carcelle before, even taken him for short dives into the upper cave, well within his limits of ability. In friendly conversation George stressed the need for considerable experience before going to the Big Room. But John had persuaded Jack, a cave diving instructor from Miami, to take him further in.

Tom and Jack were planning to explore the North Passage beyond its current limit, and George was planning to take photographs in the entrance area. Tom and Jack set off at 4.20, and would successfully lay another 500 ft (150 m) of line beyond the end of the cave. They were followed 10 minutes later by Jim and John, who intended to dive in the lower South Passage, a more dangerous lower passage below the Big Room.

When George got back in the boat at 5.00, he was told that John was missing. Jim reported that, at a depth of 180 ft (54 m), John panicked, grabbed hold of the rock wall and, despite all Jim could do, refused to be moved. Tom and Jack had learned this during their decompression stop, when Jim made it back, but by then had too little air to help. There was nothing that could be done; John would by now have breathed his tanks dry, and would be dead.

The next day, Tom and Jim entered the water at 4.20 am to recover John's body. They found it much deeper than they expected, at 255 ft (68 m), not 180 ft (54 m). John had ditched his tanks, his mask was off, his buoyancy vest was over his head and he was well off the line. His body had no obvious injuries, and it seemed that a mixture of panic and narcosis had been responsible for his death. But that is academic. Beyond a depth of 100 ft (30 m), narcosis is only one of several problems a novice may face. Rapid, shallow breathing – the epitomy of fear, can build up dangerous levels of carbon dioxide in the lungs, causing blackout. Narcosis itself heightens the effects of fear. To undertake such a difficult dive at a depth of 180 ft (54 m) inside a submarine cave so early on in a diving career is foolhardy. In this case, fatally so.

Jack took the body from them at 40 ft (12 m), while they began a 90-minute decompression, and he and George laid it on a stretcher in the boat above. John's tanks were recovered next day. On the surface, they had 200 lb (90 kg) of air pressure in them – not enough to provide enough air through the breathing regulator at 250 ft (75 m). John had been, to all intents and purposes, out of air when he died. Tom recommended that in future no one who had logged less than a hundred dives should dive in the Blue Hole. Deep cave diving was not a place for novices, however competent or daring.

Later that week, Frank Martz rejoined them. Frank was still infatuated by the idea of what lay beyond the 300 ft (90 m) mark in the great pit beyond the Grotto. He and Jim Lockwood planned a dive there for the following day. Benjamin was not amused. The dive had not been planned for that expedition, and he felt it was unsafe. His divers had their own plan for the day, and this was an unwelcome, and potentially dangerous, intrusion. Lockwood had done little to impress himself on Benjamin the week before, and Martz was intending to push the very limits of compressed air diving in a cave – the Big Pit was at least 300 ft (90 m) deep, and over 1,000 ft (300 m) inside. Their planning seemed hazy at the least. Tom disagreed, and eventually persuaded George to allow them use of the boat. George cancelled his own photographic dive, unhappy with the way the day was turning out.

The logbook entry is sad and succinct.

September 4th. 11.14 am. Frank and Jim went into South Passage. Frank did not make it out.

Frank Martz and Jim Lockwood prepare to embark on the fatal dive into Benjamin's Blue Hole. Only Lockwood will return. *(Photo: Dr George Benjamin)*

When the tragedy occurred, Tom and Zidi, another of the team, were in the North Passage, mapping it. On hearing the news on their return to the decompression point, Tom joined Jim in making a short penetration back into the South Passage, hoping vainly that Frank might reappear. But there was to be no miracle, Frank was dead, the cave's second victim in ten days. Tom and Jim pushed themselves close to the limit in their brief search, both ran out of air during decompression, and had to breathe from spare tanks brought down to them from above.

It was over an hour later before they could surface, and Jim could tell his story. He and Frank had made it back to the Grotto. Frank had attached a new reel, and gone on down. He reached a restriction at 280 ft (84 m), but negotiated this successfully, and went on down to 300 ft (90 m). There, he tied off the line. This stirred up a lot of silt, and the two divers became separated. In the fog of silt, Jim thought Frank must have gone out, and made his own way up. He never saw Frank again.

The difference between the two incidents was numbing. John had been an amateur, an inexperienced diver who should never have been where he was in the first place. Frank was one of the most experienced cave divers the United States had produced, and his death stunned the team. Tom Mount, in a statement to the police, summed up Frank's degree of experience succinctly.

Frank was probably one of the best cave divers in the world. He was a NAUI and PADI [two American diving organizations] instructor, and a NACD [National Association for Cave Divers] -certified cave diving instructor. He was one of my best friends, and one of the people you think it is impossible for them to die diving. He had done more to develop safe cave diving equipment than anyone, and the cave diving world will miss him, his abilities, his excellent diving equipment and his devotion to the exploration of underwater caves.

The Florida team were numbed by Frank's loss. Tom and Jim tried twice to find his body, descending 250 ft (75 m) in the pit. Tom was particularly upset, as the logbook entry for the second attempt shows.

Last attempt to locate Frank. Dive to 250 ft (75 m) for 25 minutes (Jim & Tom). Guess that's goodbye to a very good friend.

Jim and Tom were both very nervous at the start of the dive, and George felt it should not be made, because of the dangers involved in such a deep recovery. But Frank was Tom's best friend and he felt the dive had to be attempted. The tension between the groups upset both sides, and the Florida divers left shortly after.

That they should even contemplate diving in the cave again so soon seems difficult for those not involved to believe. Tom and Jim were obviously tremendously upset, as were George and all the others. Each showed the stress in their own way, some retreating into themselves, some more visibly upset. Faced with such sudden loss, everyone acts a little irrationally, and sometimes it is easier to follow routines until the shock wears off a little.

George returned the following month, and made a series of photographic and filming dives in Mangrove Cay and South Bight caves for *Skin Diver* magazine and a Canadian television special, and again later that year with the famous underwater photographer, Stan Waterman. He no longer worked with the Miami group, but with some of his long time friends from Canada.

The year ended with another tragedy, this time off the Wall. Archie Forfar, one of George's oldest diving companions, now ran a small diving resort at Stafford Creek. Like most of the divers in the Andros circle, he was infatuated with the Wall, and the idea of diving deeper on air than anyone else. Air-diving records, viewed objectively, are on a par with playing Russian roulette with an increasing number of bullets in the gun. The deeper you go, the more likely you are to convulse through oxygen poisoning, and die. Some people are more tolerant than others to the effects of the increase in the partial pressure of the gas. No one is immune; everyone, if they breathe it deep enough, will die.

In late 1971 Archie and his girlfriend set up an attempt off the Wall at Stafford Creek. They established a system where, in theory, they could be brought back up virtually automatically if something went wrong at the deepest point. Unfortunately, something went wrong before this, and they abandoned their escape plan. Their support diver was Sheck Exley (who went on to become America's foremost cave diver), and, at almost 500 ft (150 m), he realized that Archie and his girlfriend were in real trouble. In attempting to reach them, he too blacked out, but not before hitting his emergency inflation device. Sheck came to on his way back to the surface, deep enough to halt his ascent and decompress without getting the bends. The others were not so fortunate; unconscious, their descent continued involuntarily. They were never seen again.

George and his team continued their exploration of the Andros Holes for several years after that, but always with the same high regard for safety that they had formulated so early on, and continuously upgraded as the years passed. Of the many hundreds of cave dives made by George's team on the expeditions, not one resulted in a serious accident. Martz and Carcelle, so vastly different in experience, created their own fatal scenarios. Many of those early Blue Hole techniques became standard cave-diving practices elsewhere in the world – Benjamin's 'Crossover' valve was marketed commercially and became the US standard for cave diving, and cave divers everywhere owe a great debt to Benjamin and his team.

In 1977 Benjamin's Andros cave diving did come to an end. Piracy on the Banks around Andros, due to corrupt drug dealers seeking 'clean boats', was the final straw. George had watched the island decline for too long.

Wearing lead for diving was fine, but he felt he would develop a serious allergy to it if someone was shooting it at him.

He remembered: '. . . the old Colonial times, when the people were friendly, the lobsters were plenty, and Dom Perignon champagne was $6 a bottle. The balmy air, the leisurely life, the boating over an emerald sea – my Blue Hole exploration was only a *by-product*. Have you ever listened to Louis Morrow Gottschalk's symphony, *Night in the Tropics*? He wrote it over a hundred years ago, and it puts the old Andros just before my eyes. It changed so rapidly in the middle seventies. If the main product is gone, then the by-product also slowly disappears, as, for me, it did.'

CHAPTER FOUR

Conch Sound

D AWN TREADS the Bahamian water like a ruffled god. A flurry of rain scutters across the ocean, knocks the tops off wavelets, leaves yellow pock marks in the sand. The sullen sun eases off the horizon, throwing a pewter gleam over the silent, fluid sea. The clouds disperse, grey fades to gold, and a solitary egret calls, clear echoes raking the paralysis of the early-morning shore.

Ghost crabs scurry in silence across the sand as the last shreds of night are left to the dawn chorus of cicadas and the dull mosquito buzz. Birds chitter amongst the casurinas. Across the smooth water, past the dark, upright silhouettes of mangrove stalks, the sea heaves in a silent, monstrous surge that lifts the water in a boiling mushroom of flow.

A monster breathes. The 'Lusca' stretches, and exhales towards the dawn. His tremendous breath, drawn in over a quarter of a day, flows out in an equal spell of time. An old woman, standing by the shore with her handthrown line, watches the mound, and drags her beaten sneakers a few careful paces further along the sand.

Her eyes squint at the morning sunlight, creasing in remembrance of a fishing smack that the Lusca took, back in the last of the summer storms. The boat had been sound, made in the old way down at Lisbon Creek, a fast boat that took the wind better than many other craft. Her owner was proud of her, had paced her against many squalls. Left at anchor in the bay, the wind triumphed at last and, tearing her from her moorings in a fierce gust, filled her with sea. Low in the water, almost awash, she had been easy prey for the Lusca. He had drawn her to his hole with slow and awful breath, and sucked her down.

She looked at the boil, and, unaware of the movement, took another pace inshore. Her mind drifted on to an almost-forgotten day when she first heard the old story that she now used to scare her grandchildren. How the Lusca, hungry after a long, still summer, took a full boat and crew in the first of the sudden autumn storms, a near-hurricane that caught them unawares as they raced for the shore. The wreckage could be seen for months by those daring enough to brave the quieter moments and risk the creature's wrath by fishing close to the edge of his lair. The clear waters at the end of his exhalation left the sea like glass, and the deep void at their feet was the home of wrecks, a blue gateway to Hell.

Whatever the myths, when George Benjamin first came to the Great Blue Hole of Conch Sound, the local Bahamians thought him utterly insane to even consider diving *near* the cave.

'Mahn, you don't intend to dive down dere! Nobody go down dere; if so, he never seen again!'

George and his divers arrived on the 'boil', when the waters were pouring from the open mouth of the submarine pit. Their boatman, more than nervous, eyed the surge.

'I remind de time de Lusca stop a two-master dead in de water. He wrap' all roun' de rudder, and wid de free hands he feelin' on deck. Once de hahnd feed a mahn, dey was a flunder in de water, and bot' mahn an' Lusca gone.'

This man himself, only a few weeks earlier, had lost a dinghy and its outboard to the beast. The boat had broken free, drifted near the Hole, and the opportunist monster gulped. Now, a bit of time having elapsed, old Lusca should be ready for seconds. The boatman, a sensible sort of fellow, kept two anchors on his new vessel and these were now both firmly entrenched in the sand.

George and Tom McCollum, his diving partner, struggled into their gear. Not altogether at ease themselves, they swam through the sandy shallows to the edge of the great pit. The current pushed at them as they dropped over the edge and entered a great arena of tumbled rock and dark crevices, of arches and caverns, in which great shoals of snappers and yellow grunts moved. Shining clouds of silversides parted to let them through, then closed behind them in a shimmering mass. They tied their line to a ledge of rock, and descended through the clear outflowing water to the mouth of a huge tunnel, 80 ft (24 m) below the surface of the sea.

There, in the sands of the cavern, lay the lost boat. Beyond, the cave beckoned, an alluring void that ranged beyond the reach of their lights, from which the waters silently poured. At their backs, the sun cast a blue glow through the water, silhouetting the outline of the pit. They hung between the underworld and the overworld, on the edge of light.

They drifted to the boat. With some difficulty, they detached the heavy outboard, and tied it to their line. The boatman was more than relieved to see them return, but was absolutely dumbfounded when they hauled the line in and produced his dripping motor. This once, the Lusca had been cheated of its spoils!

Conch Sound continued to keep George and his divers in interesting times. During several visits they explored the huge tunnel with its fierce currents for over 300 ft (90 m), 80 ft (24 m) below the bay above. The walls were almost smooth, scoured by the force of the flow, and weakened by untold generations of millions of tiny creatures that made their home on the rock, boring into it for anchorage against the underwater gale.

These tiny organisms – sponges, anemones, corals – were not the only inhabitants of the cave. Many creatures used the darkness for shelter, or for a secure home. Then there were the sharks.

George and George Junior, with Archie Forfar and Heinz Bolliger, decided one day to photograph the huge cave by the light of several big underwater strobes. They swam into the cave, strung out in a line with George at the rear, camera poised. Suddenly, out of the gloom ahead, two large sharks came silently towards them.

Being met by such a sight in the open sea would have been nerve-racking enough, but in a cave . . .? The sharks moved excitedly, nervously, startled by the lights. They swerved, and moved back into the cave. The only thing worse than meeting a shark in such a place is making it feel trapped. A rat in a corner has got nothing on a shark in a similar position. One of the sharks made a break for the entrance, but, having passed the first divers, it saw George and darted back again towards the others. Suddenly all George could see was a whirl of brown silt from which swung arms, fins, cables and the shark's tail. Being a good camerman, he pointed the camera and pressed the trigger. Nothing happened: the cables had broken in the maul, and the flash was out of action.

> It was not the one in front of me, that I could see, that was bothering me, but the one behind me, sharing this cloud of silt. Suddenly, I was sure I felt something nibbling my fin. At that moment it didn't matter whether it was a shark, or just my imagination!

The sharks disappeared into the darkness inside the cave. Shaken, Benjamin's team retreated, leaving the unexpected monsters to their lair. Later, when George developed the film, he found that Heinz had been so close to the shark that, even without the flash, his floodlight had allowed an acceptable picture of the beast – Heinz had actually been shoving the shark away with it!

Shortly after this episode, they decided there were better things down south. Conch Sound was left to the Lusca and its sleek, silent companions.

The thin yellow cord snaked out of sight, away into the distance beyond the beam of light. I swam through a world of strange and mysterious shapes, haunted by scuttling crabs and wraith-like eels, a thousand feet from day. Around me, half-buried stalagmites grew out of sculpted dunes, for all the world like broken pillars of some drowned and forgotten city, lost beneath

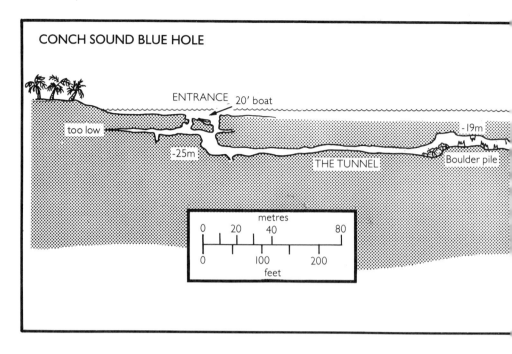

the sea. Across this Atlantean landscape, two bright lights glowed in the distance, adding perspective to the cave.

Floating in mid-water at the end of the line, Martyn Farr waited for me. For several days, diving sometimes twice each day, we had been exploring Conch Sound Blue Hole. Now, having traversed over 600 ft (180 m), we had entered a desert of perpetual night, where vast dunes faded into nebulous landscapes at the edge of vision. I tied my reel of line on to the end of Martyn's, and swam on with a brief nod of acknowledgement. This had become our standard procedure, each leap-frogging the other as our reels ran out. Our only link with the outside world was this thin cord that stretched back along the many hundreds of feet to the great, chaotic entrance crater, over 40 minutes' swim away.

Martyn moved in behind, a reassuring presence. The passage here was too large for our lights fully to penetrate. We swam into a continuous mist, pausing only to tie the line to occasional detached blocks or the odd group of stalagmites. These rose like fairy-tale castles from the sand, islands in the submarine desert providing the only break in the relentless journey into the unknown, a place to pause and reorientate oneself. At length, my line ran out, and I tied it to a stalagmite tower. We waited a moment, checking the array of gauges that showed the air reserves in each of the three separate breathing systems we carried, then turned and began the long swim out that would traverse the length of the cave again before we could take the

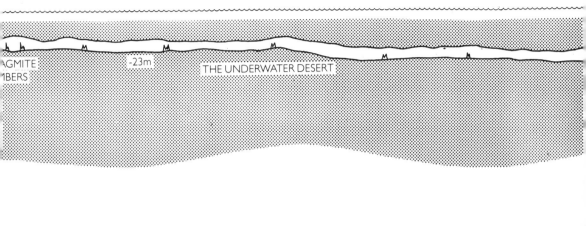

regulators from our mouths and breathe fresh air. Only 70 ft (20 m) above our heads, the sun shone on the waves, and birds called across the bay. Those few feet were solid rock; there was no easy way out.

As cave divers reared in the cold, barren caves of Britain, Blue Holes fascinated us. The life, the beauty of submerged grottoes, the size, and the sheer mystery of the caves themselves – all went to make Bahamian caves more spectacular than any mud-filled British offering. Here was an exploratory challenge equal to anything; the discovery and exploration of a 'lost world' beneath the sea.

As it happened, our first dive in Conch Sound was almost our last. We were acolytes, third day on the island, ready for anything. Martyn and I kitted up on the beach 100 yards from the Blue Hole, with two 80 cu. ft (6.8 cu. m) tanks apiece, more than enough air for the length of line we carried. A short dive in the entrance the day before had showed us the cave mouth where Benjamin had found the Lusca's boat over a decade ago, and we knew the depth to expect. The currents, we'd decided, would stop inflowing 2½ hours after high tide on the surface. We were going to be clever, and ride the last of the inflow, using it to carry us into the cave, and therefore saving effort and air. By timing our dive perfectly, we could then ride the growing outflow the other way. We were pleased with ourselves, full of the confidence of the uninitiated.

Behind us, George Warner, our biologist, would be working in the

CONCH SOUND BLUE HOLE

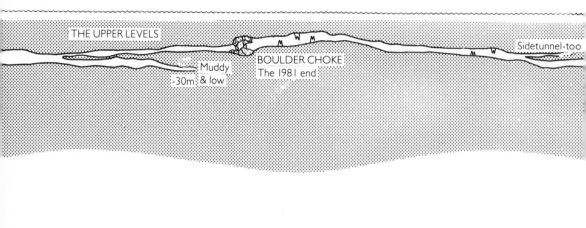

THE UPPER LEVELS

Muddy
-30m & low

BOULDER CHOKE
The 1981 end

Sidetunnel-too

entrance area of the cave, studying the complex community of marine life
that graced the walls, roof and floor. The current that flowed into the cave
carried food with it – enough to provide a free lunch twice a day for the
sessile animals that clung to every available surface. Rod Beaumont, the
third cave diver in our party, intended to hang around the entrance area
until he was a little more familiar with the environment. He was the only
one among us with any sense.

We made our final checks at the mouth of the cave. The current was still
flowing in strongly; the ride would be a fast one. Off we went, soaring into
the cave, barely moving our fins – and then only to steer. Occasionally we
paused, to tie the line securely to solid outcrops of rock, probably the only
sensible thing we did that day.

Three hundred feet inside the cave, the first reel ran out near a huge rock
pillar that split the passage into two. A group of interested crawfish watched
warily from a crevice in the wall as we tied the line off, and attached the
second reel. The flow seemed to be slackening as we swam on, following the
enormous underwater tunnel into the gloom ahead. At 500 ft (150 m), still
80 ft (24 m) down, a chaotic tumble of rocks formed an underwater
barricade across the cave. Black space opened above, and we rose, to
emerge into a huge cavern. In front of us, stalagmites reared from the floor,
pillars of stone that had long ago lost their crystal sheen and were now
covered by long centuries of marine concretion and animal growth that

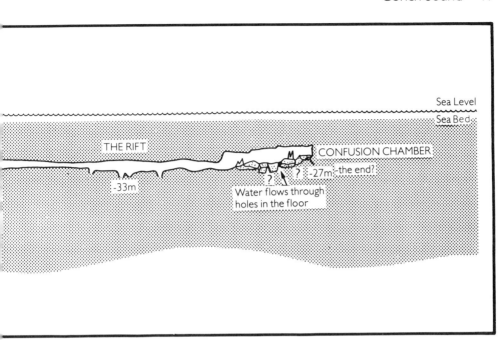

camouflaged their dripstone origin. Their shape was enough. On our first real dive in an Andros Blue Hole, we had discovered the formations that George Benjamin and his team has spent so long searching for. Had they only known that a few hundred feet further in one of the first caves they had explored . . .

I turned to Martyn, and proudly wrote on my slate, 'Stalagmites'.

'Really . . .? Very clever!' his eyes said sarcastically.

We grinned at each other, and laid out the last remaining feet of line, attaching the end triumphantly to a stalagmite in the middle of the chamber, 600 ft (180 m) from the surface. With a last look into the darkness ahead, we turned to go.

And found the current was still flowing in. Fast.

Finning against it was almost out of the question. I can clearly remember looking at my gauges after the first 100 ft (30 m), panting for air, and thinking that this might be it. I thanked whatever God was watching us that day that we'd used a strong line, that was thick enough to pull on, because I broke the rule that says you mustn't pull on the line almost all the way out. It would have been impossible to swim without it . . . sometimes I tried pulling myself along the rough floor, but it broke away in lumps in my hands as the current pushed against me. Dimly in the distance, and very slowly, the entrance came closer. My gauges edged towards the red. At last, as the passage spread out to greet the light, I could let go of the line and rise towards the surface to decompress, and breathe freely again. Self-confidence crept into a corner, curled up, and shivered.

George had had an even worse time. Entranced by the life on the walls, he hadn't realized that the current was taking him deeper and deeper into the cave. Eventually he remembered to look at his gauges, and realized where he was – and that the current was against him. Only his considerable diving experience got him out – virtually as his tank breathed dry. Rod was at the surface as he emerged, gasping and shaken. George wasn't a cave diver . . . he shouldn't have been so far in on his own. We all learnt big lessons that day.

Several dives later, more confident and more experienced, we were back at the end of the cave. The line rattled sharply from the reel as the last few coils spun out. A small flake on the right-hand wall coincided with the final tug on the cord. Something had subtly changed in the cave. The floor was fine silt, the roof lowering towards it. The clouds of sediment stirred up by our movements hung torpidly, with little enthusiasm for flowing in any particular direction. I put it down to slack water, the cave currents must be about to reverse. Martyn was back down the passage a little, higher in the roof, looking at something. He joined me as I cut the empty reel free and turned, ready to begin the 2,000 ft (600 m) swim back to daylight and clean, fresh air.

The current mounted as we swam back, slowly at first, then quickening in strength and effect, making finning irrelevant. We floated effortlessly through the stalagmite halls, and down over the boulder barrier into the entrance tunnel. Gathering speed, we swept down an underwater roller-coaster that, when we allowed attention to lapse momentarily, bounced us mercilessly off the abrasive coral walls. Submarine Jacks, with seven league fins, we were spat into daylight on an adrenalin high, rejected again by that giant mythical octopus, the Lusca.

Decompressing in the latest of the monster's titbits, a 20 ft (6 m) motorboat, we idly watched small fish defend their acquired crannies against our teasing fingers, launching used tanks at the surface as we breathed them close to dry.

Later, stripping our suits off in the sunlight on the beach, a grizzled old Bahamian wandered up, full of curiosity and native knowledge.

'Dat hole, mahn, it go all de way to Nassau. Dat true. Mr Benjamin, he swim there.' We hid grins. He told us the story of the Lusca and the engine, gloriously embellished by ten years of folklore. It seemed that local legend has still to come to terms with the basics of geology – a cave 6,000 ft (1,800 m) deep and 40 miles (64 km) long that cut under the Tongue of the Ocean to reappear in the Bahamian capital would be a story indeed!

Ending his tale with a two-arm flourish towards the horizon, several degrees south of Nassau, he pointed more accurately across the bay.

'There another boilin' hole there, out in de bay. My grandson, dis him,' he said, tugging a poor unfortunate nine-year-old fondly but firmly by an ear, 'he take you theah.'

Even from a distance it was obvious. The van was abandoned at the end of the track, and a short walk through mangrove swamp brought us to a small bay, an inlier of the main Conch Sound. There was a dramatic mound of water 200 ft (60 m) or so offshore, mushrooming through the waves that swept into the bay. We waded out, and peered at the upwelling flow. The outflow was cold, and a strong smell of sulphur filled the air. Around the 6 ft (1.8 m)-diameter entrance, the seabed was covered by a pallid algal matting, unlike anything we had seen at a Blue Hole before. We looked at each other with wide eyes, daunted, and well-impressed!

CHAPTER FIVE

The Inland Cenotes and Conch Sound Two

*P*OCK MARKED by great circular pools and algal-floored oolitic ponds, the west coast of Andros is a different world entirely. Vast acres of desolation, like a wild, post-holocaust landscape, stretch beyond the last stands of pine forest, fading through scrubby wilderness into an indeterminable littoral zone of tidal ponds, shallow, rambling creeks, and scattered, twisted mangroves. Here is isolation indeed. The only sounds are the cry of birds, the winds brushing softly across the landscape, and the occasional scuffle from the warm liquid creek as water birds or turtles disturb the silence.

Butterflies and great iridescent dragonflies flitter from shrubs to orchids, bright flowering stabs of blue that wind around the twisted wrecks of dead, parched trees. Occasionally, soaring in from its aerial fish-scan, an osprey swoops to a high branch, surveying the wasteland. Pelicans, or a rare flock of pink flamingos, are the glamour in the wilderness, the bright aristocracy of desolation row.

The mangroves spread relentlessly, reclaiming the oolitic sands from the shallow sea, turning them slowly to dry land. This process is aeons old, a slow march that began when the Bahamas first rose above the waves, occasionally interrupted by tempest, hurricane, or, every few thousand years, by a sly trick of nature as the slight warming of the polar ice brings seas rising in slow acknowledgement, inundating the flatlands. The islands shiver in response, shrinking in on themselves as the ocean encroaches. Then the poles cool, the ice freezes again, and the mangroves recommence their subtle march to reclaim earth from sea. The Bahamas are the 'Ephemeral Islands', a transient landscape that rides the waves with an undaunted tenacity that seems to say 'I am born, I shall survive.'

Further inland, in the increasing gap between the creeks, small stands of coppice appear. Birds nest in their shelter, *anolis* lizards scurry in their undergrowth, crabs burrow into holes where rain has eaten cavities in the limestone rock. These small isolated clumps of brushland thicken and gather together the further one proceeds inland from the coast. Where the rock rises far enough above the level of the sea to support a thin lens of freshwater, the thick broadleaved coppice turns to tall forests of Caribbean pine.

Scattered throughout the landscape, like coins in a fountain, are the circular shapes of inland Blue Holes. Out in the oolitic flats, their dark-blue outlines are fringed with a halo of tiny tributary streamlets, stylized azure suns laid flat in a sky of sand. Their levels rise and fall with the tides, alternately pouring water out across the landscape, or draining the brackish streamlets back into the underground world beneath the Bahamas. It may be that some of this water flows deep, passing underneath the island, to emerge a long time later from ocean Holes inside the fringing reef on the eastern shore. But the west coast Holes are isolated, there are no roads, no paths, sometimes even no creeks that come remotely near them. We do not know what lies in their depths.

More accessible are the circular blue gems in the pine forests themselves. During the 1950s and 1960s, Andros was logged, the pine forests cut to make paper and pit-props, the landscape criss-crossed by logging tracks bulldozed to access the remotest corners of the pine woods. Doubtless it was hot, hard work . . . many of the tracks end conveniently near Blue Holes, and it is easy to imagine a sweating bulldozer driver altering his path to head for the cold blue lake behind the next grove of trees.

What effect this plundering of Andros's resources had on its wildlife, we may never know. Rumours of 'Chickcharnies', mythical three-toed elves that lived in nests in trees, are still common on Andros. The giant barn owls that were the probable originators of the myth are now extinct, but it would be sad to think that the last possible nesting grounds of these once common Bahamian birds were unknowingly destroyed by this latest avaricious grasp at the land. Wild pigs, escapees from village pens, now roam the interior of North Andros, visually indistinguishable from the wild boars of their ancestry. They, and man, have between them seen off most of the remaining rock iguanas, the giant Bahamian lizard that grew to lengths of five feet and more. Those that remain dwell mainly in the south, in scattered coppices or isolated stands of pine where pigs and man rarely go.

The inland Blue Holes are utterly different from the bustling, living caves out on the reef. They have a quiet sanctity, an aloofness, an awesomeness far different from that generated by the fierce currents and twisting corridors of the coastal caves. Set in rings of coppice within the tall pines, their walls dropping vertically beneath fragile strands of algae and bacterial mat, they plummet straight, unequivocably, down into the bowels of Andros.

As a bad-weather alternative to ocean Holes, Benjamin's group took advantage of the new accessibility and set about exploring the deep inland lakes. To Archie Forfar, these became an especial fascination, their clear, silent waters beckoning in total contrast to the bright, humid heat on the surface. They were windows into the aquifer, into the deep freshwater 'lenses' that lay beneath the main part of North Andros, perhaps the island's greatest remaining resource. In some Holes the freshwater layer is thin, the interface with the underlying saltwater lying only a few feet down. In others, the halocline, the mixing zone between the two waters, lay over 100 ft (30 m) below the forest above. In the early 1970s a British hydrological survey plumbed many of them, using helicopters to reach the more remote Holes. Some of those they plumbed were over 360 ft (108 m) deep.

Of the many inland holes Benjamin's team dived, there was an outstanding favourite. Benjamin called it simply 'Archie's Blue Hole', in memory of the man who died only a few days after Benjamin had filmed him in its depths, on a final adventure into the deep waters of the Tongue of the Ocean.

Archie's Blue Hole lies near the abandoned plantation and airstrip at Twin Lakes, now a place to avoid, the illicit haunt of drug-runners. In 1981 Ken and Laurie Jones, two of the divemasters at the Forfar Field Station, found themselves spreadeagled on the ground with shotguns at their heads, in the hands of a group of obviously unfriendly individuals who suggested they might like not to appear unannounced again. The twin lakes of the plantation's name are themselves deep blue holes, and the ruins a legacy of Neville Chamberlain's disastrous attempts at sisal farming, as a result, say the Androsians, of this having angered the Chickcharnies by cutting down their nests.

Archie's Hole lies a few miles north, a safe distance from the plantation site, near the end of a small side track off the main logging highway. In Archie's day the tracks were new and the drive was easy, now the roads are partially overgrown and many of the Holes are virtually inaccessible once again. 'Archie's' is easier to get to than most, and, while a relatively safe dive, is one of the most spectacular and unearthly experiences a diver could hope for.

Like most of the inland Holes, the lake is surrounded by a thin halo of coppice woodland, wherein orchids, cacti, creeping vines and bright flowers compete for space on the rock by the water's edge. The edge drops abruptly, the rock below water is hidden beneath a coating of fine algae, hanging in strange, unearthly fronds that give the Hole a haunted and ghostly atmosphere. Sinking deeper, daylight fades and the walls fall away, belling out into a massive underground dome. The rock emerges, fretted by solution into the texture of a fine limestone sponge. Though the light has dimmed, visibility is 50 ft (15 m) and more, more than enough to gain a feeling for the awesome immensity of the place. There is a sensation of weightless flight, as you hover in front of the great rock walls that slope up and down, and out from side to side, beyond vision, that is entirely different from the deep open sea. Here, where the boundaries are invisible, there is the impression of a great enclosure, you are inside a world, a mote in the eye of a God.

The real wonder lies below 70 ft (20 m), on the north side of the cavern. Here, beneath an overhang, great mudstone stalactites 20 ft (6 m) and more in length hang down towards the unseen floor below. The gnarled, convoluted surfaces of the stalactites bear evidence to their formation – these are not great rock crystals, formed of pure limestone, but the relics of sea-levels 100 ft (30 m) or so lower than today, when muddy waters dripped down roots, or down great strands of vines. Congealing slowly into these inverted stone pillars as the drips evaporated in the heat, the muds coated the substance below with a thickening layer of stone.

All the great mudstone stalactites end around the 100 ft (30 m) mark. This may have been the level at which the waters stood while the formations were growing, when the lake and the Hole looked much like one of the great *cenotes* still to be seen in the Yucatan peninsula of northern Mexico. Or they may be responding to the curious phenomena that lies today at the −100 ft (−30 m) level, where the 'mixing zone' between the freshwater above and the saltwater below occurs.

Hitting the mixing zone in Archie's Hole is a curious experience – one that Benjamin likened to bouncing off a trampoline. Saltwater is denser than fresh; things that sink through the upper waters hit the mixing zone, and stop. This includes much of the organic material that falls into the wide diameter of the surface hole. Here at the mixing zone, bacteria break this down, and this generates heat. The bacterial layer colours the water a dull orange, and its activity generates a mild sulphuric acid, with a very distinctive 'rotten eggs' taste. All this, combined with the general atmosphere of the cathedral-like underwater *cenote*, tends to make the mixing zone the final straw, the turn-round point for the exploring diver.

The intermingling densities caused when a diver disturbs the water further serve to heighten the sense of unease, the distinction of a boundary between the known world and something else. For those with nerve enough to penetrate below the sulphur layer, there comes an additional, and not too pleasant, a surprise. The bacterial layer eats light too – the water beneath it is black as midnight, but its clarity is astonishing. With no light, there is no algal bottom, for no photosynthesis is possible. There are no currents to disturb the silt; there is no activity. Here, there are no seasons, no day, no light. This is a real underworld, the waters of Lethe, the silent zone. The sulphur layer is a tangible barrier, a wall between dimensions, the boundary between the world we know and a world of eternal darkness still enough to clutch at your very soul.

The first time I dived alone through it, reluctantly, to snatch a sample of the deep, dark waters of Archie's Cave, I hung close to the wall, focusing almost desperately on its rough, fretted surface. The walls ended 120 ft down (36 m) in a bank of silt, a fine black powdery dune that swept in a downward curve towards the unseen depths in the centre of the Hole. Alone, and inexperienced, I was too close to the borderland, the twilight area of unconscious fear, submerged by atavistic memories of primeval night. It was dark, and lonely, and immense. I was enclosed in liquid, weightless, with no sense of up, or down. There was no sound, only my jagged breathing and the metallic explosion of air through the regulator. My tank struck the wall, and the hollow ring echoed dully, eerily. My fingers, groping blindly, hit the inflation button on my buoyancy vest. Air flowed in with a scream, I rose, and tasted the vile decay of the sulphur layer as light and warmth returned to my world. I floated by the stalactites, tense, and shivering with more than cold. It wasn't a pleasant experience, first time, and alone.

Hanging in the freshwater, seeing and feeling the rays of the sun as it lanced through the green shallows, allowed adrenalin to submerge the fear, allowed me to stretch in delight at the experience, turning my body in a twisting somersault of emotion. I was alive, I had experienced a new and delicious sensation that had stimulated me in all my senses. I felt as though I had pressed beyond life and returned, gone out of the world and come back. Surely nothing else could intimidate me now!

Resting my helmet on the dark limestone surface, I quietly asked my ego why it had brought me there. Two rock walls gripped me tightly between them, in the claustrophobic darkness of an underwater cave, 90 ft (27 m) below the surface of the sea. Cream-coloured muck floated in the water, knocked from the walls by my struggles, and borne past me by a rapidly mounting current. Somewhere off to one side, out of view, was a narrow gap that led out of the underwater cave, back to the oh-so-distant Bahamian sunshine somewhere above.

Unfortunately there were few clues as to where 'out' was. I'd been moving up too quickly, trying to get out of the cave before the current grew strong enough to flush me somewhere I didn't want to be. The guideline laid so casually on the inward trip, down what had seemed like a wide-open rift, now paid back such incaution. It had slipped sideways into a narrowing of the crack, and my off-track ascent had wedged me into a space too tight to pass.

I tried wriggling backwards, but the side-mounted tanks on my hips caught on flakes of rock, and stopped me descending. At that depth, air supplies were dwindling quickly; each breath used three times as much air as at the surface, due to the greater pressure of the water around me. Even worse, my partner, Martyn Farr, was still somewhere beneath me and unaware of my predicament – and so I had to sort things out before it became *our* predicament!

An hour earlier we had been cursing the rain on the surface. The Bahamas mean sunshine – or so say all the brochures! Thunder and lightning never appear in the pictures, but they cracked the atmosphere that morning, as we struggled through the tangle of mangroves fringing the rocky south shore of Conch Sound. Rod Beaumont trudged resignedly through the shallow sea with 40 lb (18 kg) of steel diving tanks on his shoulder as the heavens roared and lightning silhouetted the queuing thunderheads across to the horizon.

The whirlpool at the entrance to the small submarine cave gradually spun more slowly as we slipped into our wetsuits on the shore nearby. Harnesses of nylon webbing held to our sides, two air tanks each with its own separate regulator to breathe through. An equipment failure deep in the cave might otherwise leave us with no air to breathe and a rock roof above our heads barring a quick getaway. Rod stood waist-deep in the warm water beside the cave – 'Conch Sound Two', the small Blue Hole across the bay from the great cave of Conch Sound. As the last flurry of raindrops spattered the water around, the sun and the flies emerged. We waded across from the shore, hauling fins, line reels and helmets through the shallow lagoon to the cave.

Most Blue Holes play home to hordes of fish, to waving hydroids and colourful sponges. This Hole was strangely different; instead of the usual marine community, the sea-floor around its maw was encircled by pallid algae, a pale wreath of soft, clammy growth caused by the sulphurous water that flowed from the Hole. The inflowing tide was clear, warmed only by the sun, carrying seaweed and small plankton into the cave. The outflow was cold, a chill that shivered exposed skin, the temperature of the darkness deep within the island. The outflow was also sulphurous, draining decaying organic material from the mangroves behind the beaches. The taint of rotting vegetation hung over the cave, like some direct route to Mephistopheles himself, an aquatic entrance to hell.

I tied the line to a rock bulge beneath the pale growth in the twilight mouth. The current flow slackened to a gentle pull, the last fading tug of the inflow. Finning carefully, trying not to fill the water with flakes of the fragile white matter, I moved slowly into the underworld. Martyn followed a few feet behind.

For 30 ft (9 m) the cave ran almost horizontally, dipping slightly into the rock below the bay. White anemones, as pallid as the algae, gestured with beckoning tentacles. A small grotto of stunted, decaying stalactites hung over a vertical void at the end of the passage. The cave went down, into the earth. Pale walls slunk away from my lights, falling into invisibility. Purging air from my buoyancy vest, I looked at Martyn, shrugged, and went down.

Committed to the cave, some of the original concern disappeared. Just another Blue Hole. A bit unusual, maybe more of a 'grey hole', but really just another void in the rock. The depth gauge crept round: 60 ft (18 m), 70 ft (21 m). Line spun, rattling, from the reel. One hundred feet . . .

I crunched on to the sandy floor 127 ft (38 m) below the surface, still in a dark and narrow canyon, but one which now seemed to run horizontally. In the shadows before me, in tune with the ambience of the dive, lay the rotting skeleton of a huge turtle. Sand ran in the eyeholes of the skull. The shell, empty, lay nearby, a mockery of brown on the white sand of the cave.

As I moved towards it the water shimmered, and the temperature plunged. Cold waves shivered across my skin. Startled, I moved back. Cautiously, forward again. The same effect. Behind the shell of the turtle, a small passage, too low to enter, poured cold water into the cave. The sudden clarity was astonishing. So was the sudden temperature drop. The eerie combination had a simple meaning . . . the current was reversing, the cave tide was about to flow out.

My reel emptied its last few turns of line, and Martyn tied his on. We exchanged nervous glances. The outflowing tide at this Hole was frightening; it poured out into the bay in a cold mushroom of water, boiling to the surface of the sea with astonishing ferocity. If we stayed too long, such unremitting force might be enough to blast us from the cave before we could stop to decompress. We had hoped to have longer during slack water than we apparently were going to have. We couldn't go much further. I belayed the line to the wall as Martyn moved off sideways into the milky underworld. I checked the air in my tanks and turned to follow but his lights met me only a few feet on, emerging from a cloud of white silt. Half-seen hands motioned signs, a brief pantomime showed he was as nervous as I about continuing. The current was a great unknown, and the character of the cave had bled our bravado like a surgeon's leech. Leaving Martyn to cut the reel free and tie the final end to the wall, I turned to make my way out.

Passing the skeleton and moving up the rift, I could feel the chill of the outflow again. Our canyon beyond the bones must have been an 'oxbow', a backwater in which the currents had little effect. I had no need to swim upwards, the cold current was now moving me on its own. The thick line snaked ahead, and I clung to it, secure in the knowledge that it would guide me out, and that it was well tied down below. If necessary, I would 'abseil' upwards, using the strength of the blue cord to combat the force of the current. At that moment, in all the confidence of error, I stuck.

Terror sat by my shoulder, and waited patiently. I closed my eyes and tried to sense the cave around me, to feel its shape, to get some psychic message from the rock. Movement back was impossible, my air tanks jammed, and the passage was too narrow for me to reach down to free them. Bubbles bounced off the walls from my regulator, confusing my vision, hiding the cave behind a screen of grey snow. I closed my eyes, breathed deeply, and banished all thoughts from my mind other than the one that said, simply, 'Live!'

Barely ten days before, on my first real exploratory dive into a Blue Hole, I had stumbled across the long dead body of an American diver. His decaying body was too vivid a memory. It came to me again that he had lacked what I had – a lifeline out. I could still move sideways, and one direction *must* lead to the widening of the rift, to the canyon we had descended on our way in. I had no idea how much air I had left, there was no chance of seeing my gauges, and I still had to decompress. Time distorted. It seemed an eternity since I'd jammed myself. I felt I would only have one good chance, and Martyn was still behind me. He would surely be on his way up now, and the thought of moving the wrong way, of consigning both of us to a partnership with the skeleton below, cleared my mind. One chance. I thrust into the mists to the right, scraping tanks and knees on the walls of the cave, breathing far too heavily. My hands clawed sideways at tiny, unseen crevices in the rock, scrabbling for any holds available. Chest and back snagged on the uneven rock, flakes tore loose and fell.

The passage widened. I floated.

Free.

Lights came up beneath me, and Martyn gave a casual wave. I nodded weakly back, and moved on up, following the blue cord towards the day.

Even then, we had to spend half-an-hour clinging for grim death to the line at the entrance, as the current streamed us horizontally out of the mouth. We fluttered like flags on the line, inching nervously back to our changing 'stop' depths. It was a battering, physical decompression: neither of us would have relished trying to struggle back to our safe depth had our grip broken. Eventually, well-shaken by the flow but with blood clear of bubbles, we could let go and fly the last few feet. We broke surface like dolphins and the sounds of life rushed in, to bathe us in reality. I had a long, long look at the sky. Blue is a wonderful colour.

The discovery of the dead American had come during the few days of the 1981 expedition, on an opportunistic dive before picking up the rest of the team at the San Andros airfield. Ken and Laurie Jones drove me north past the airport, and we turned into a small side track through the forest to Uncle Charlie's Blue Hole, a small inland Hole regularly used by the Forfar Station for swimming in. There were rumours of cave passages leading off, but Ken had dived there several times and seen nothing. We were diving there in the hopes of finding a blind cave fish called *Lucifuga*, discovered in New Providence, but as yet unknown on Andros. This was the sort of place it might be, shallow, clear, and with many small crevices to sneak back into.

Uncle Charlie's was a very pretty place. Surrounded by a 6 ft high cliff, the entry to the water was delightful, a leap into cool enveloping fluid that purged the heat of the surface forest immediately. We swam the circumference of the pool, chasing frogs and crabs, and swimming in and out of old tree trunks 20 ft (9 m) down. And there, in pockets round the sides of the pool where tiny caves led off, we found *Lucifuga*, our blind cave fish, a distant relative of marine 'brotulids', shy fish which hide in crevices within the reef or in small caves in overhangs and drop-offs. Clear candidates for cave adaptation, their ancestors may have been trapped by falling sea levels. Or perhaps they simply retreated further into the fissure system beneath the islands, leaving the dangerous hunting grounds of the reef for a more tranquil existence in the total darkness of underwater caves inside Bahamian rock. Perhaps this latter explanation is the best; we have often seen them since in the distant reaches of marine caves, and they could easily migrate from inland hole to ocean hole through the maze of fissures beneath the islands.

We casually worked our way down the rocky slopes of the cave, past stands of fossil coral etched in the rock, where the organic waters had dissolved softer limestones from around the hard, calcareous skeletons of ancient reefs, to the soft silt of the bottom of the entrance lake. Our lights made out a trench in the floor, right in the centre of the Hole, and we floated down into the maw of the cave. The waters turned orange, and a sulphurous taste crept past our mouthpieces. The walls were repulsive and loose – I thrust my arm into the decaying 'mung', and it disappeared to the elbow. Visibility fell to a couple of feet, just enough to see Ken's light a little above me. Just as I was getting apprehensive about continuing down without a line I came out, suddenly and unexpectedly, into perfect visibility and a rock-walled chamber. Ken and Laurie were still above me, their lights glowing dimly through the sulphur layer. I rose quickly, gave Ken the end of the small line reel I carried, and made firm 'stay where you are' motions. Ken made an OK sign, and I sank down to explore. The cave continued, straight on down, but an obvious passage led off one side. Twenty feet (6 m) in, the passage emerged in the side of a larger cavern, a rift that continued north as far as I could see, though there appeared to be a boulder obstruction on the right.

A glint in the roof caught my eye. I looked up. A torch hung from a cord, in front of me. I wondered foolishly for a moment how Ken had managed to find another way in. Then I looked up. High in the rift, wedged firmly in the rock, hung the tattered remnants of a previous explorer. His wetsuit, torn and misshapen, held what was left of him together, though bones emerged through the tears. I could clearly make out the gear he wore, and tried to avoid staring directly into the mask that looked towards me, the head bowed as though in final acceptance of death.

At first I had a strange, fleeting feeling of disappointment at the obvious fact that I wasn't the first to find this cave, a sensation that soon turned to a great sadness at the fate that must have befallen the diver above. I felt no horror at being enclosed with a long-dead corpse, just a sorrow that this man had died attempting to do the very things I so loved doing. The sorrow was a stronger emotion than fear, and I sadly reeled the line back through the clouds of fine silt that utterly obscured the way back out, to tell the others of my find. They were still waiting at the bottom of the trench, below the sulphur layer, and we ascended together, talked briefly on the surface, and climbed out of the Hole.

We drove back to the airfield, trying to piece together what might have happened. The diver wore only one tank, though with an 'octopus' regulator, where two mouthpieces came from one first stage on the tank.

Cool subterranean waters well out of the azure entrance to Rat Cay Blue Hole. *(Photo: Dr George Benjamin)*

In the Grotto of Benjamin's Blue Hole, divers of George Benjamin's team discovered massive dripstone formations that indicated that the caves, for part of their existence, lay above water. *Photo: Dr George Benjamin)*

In the underwater tunnels beneath the South Bight of Andros, cave diver's lights pick out stalagmite formations, relics of an age when the caves stood clear of the waves. *(Photo: Dr George Benjamin)*

Set in a surrounding reef of coral growth, the gaping maw of Shark Hole on South Andros could well be the haunt of the mysterious 'Lusca'. *(Photo: Rob Palmer)*

The unfathomed depths of the kilometre-wide Black Hole pierce the flat Bahamian landscape. A halo of shrubbery is an indication of fresher water, but this huge underwater cavern is still unexplored. *(Photo: Rob Palmer)*

Deep in the underwater passages of Conch Sound Blue Hole, Rob Palmer follows the guideline across the submarine dunes towards an island of stalagmites. *(Photo: Martyn Farr)*

Thick tropical bush straggles down the vertical cliffs of inland Blue Holes near Deep Creek, to reach the water's edge. Biologist John Hutchison searches for dragonflies which flutter across the extensive algal beds. *(Photo: Paul Stewart)*

Barbouria cubensis, a Caribbean cave-shrimp found in many of the South Andros Blue Holes. These brightly-coloured shrimps eat virtually any organic material floating down into the cave waters, from dead vegetation to large water-dwelling beetles. *(Photo: Rob Palmer)*

Two of the tiny jellyfish from El Dorado and Jellyfish Lake. These tiny medusae swim in their tens of thousands in the dim cavern waters. *(Photo: Chris Howes FRPS)*

Bill Stone and Rob Palmer prepare to dive in El Dorado, each wearing cylinders filled with air and heliox for the deep dive ahead. *(Photo: Chris Howes FRPS)*

Rob Palmer approaches El Puerto del Diablo in El Dorado. *(Photo: Bill Stone)*

This itself was woefully inadequate for cave diving; a failure in one part of the breathing system still means that all the air can escape from the tank. Trained cave divers always use at least two separate systems, where a failing part can be isolated before all the air is lost. He appeared to have carried only one torch, and it may be that had failed, blinding him. But the probable answer was a different sort of blindness; without the reel of line to guide me out, I too might have ended up like the long-dead diver, caught in the confines of the cave with no method of finding my point of entry as the clouds of silt rolled in to eclipse his life. His air bubbles, the movements of his hands and fins, the simple wake of his passage all created eddies in the water that dislodged tiny particles of rock and silt from the walls, the roof, the floor of the cave. Groping blindly in the darkness, his torch useless and unable to pierce the floating silt-storm, he could only rely on touch to find his way. Sadly his groping fingers found only a blind rift, a rising dead-end in which he breathed his air out, and died. By breaking a few simple rules – two breathing sets, two or more lights, a guideline – he lost the game.

Wedged in the roof of Uncle Charlie's Blue Hole, the body of an unfortunate American diver bears witness to the extreme dangers of underwater cave exploration. *(Photo: Martyn Farr)*

We picked the rest of the team up from the airport, and drove back to Forfar. There, we told them of our find, a cold sobering beginning to our explorations in the Blue Holes of Andros.

CHAPTER SIX

Doughnuts and disagreements

MEMORIES OF high spots in life are always vivid. Sunlight dancing in the water, flickering shadows and golden glowing leaves on the kelp bed off the Northumbrian beach where I first swam with the freedom of a facemask and clear sight beneath the sea. The instant love of this new world, a weightless world of light, where the slippery fronds of seaweed that made walking the rocky shoreline treacherous became a forest through which small silver fish flew like birds, and red crabs grazed like armoured animals, scurrying in alarm into the sheltering kelp as the shadow overhead grew too big to be weed.

Memories of the first time I swam in an underwater cave, beneath the lower slopes of Littondale, in Yorkshire. The absolute commitment of entering an environment in which I, the man-animal, could not breathe, could not easily run away to surface if I failed, could not see beyond the range of the small underwater lights I carried, could depend only on a rubber and metal artefact clutched in my teeth to keep me alive. The crashing of the air in the valve in the muffling silence of the cave, the translucence of the water, the rolling clouds of silt that rose behind, and the artificial curve of the orange cord that connected more sensible corners of the world together, places full of air that I could breathe. And the utter relief of surfacing, the joy of being There and being Then, a surge of young adrenalin that said how good it was to have adventure, and to really live! There are few more rewarding experiences than offering all you have to the altar of chance and skill, committing life itself to the walk along the wire, and emerging whole on the other side. The world smells more vibrant, the colours bear a richer, truer glow, you are so utterly aware of it all, and of its astonishing worth.

So it was when I first dived the Wall, hanging alone, 200 ft (60 m) below the distant silhouette of the boat, floating 50 ft (15 m) away from the edge of the giant underwater cliff that faded into blueness far below, curving out to underwater foothills 2,000 ft (600 m) down. Deep shafts of sunlight followed the curve of the rock, lending perspective to the giant tubes of sponges, the coiling whips of black coral, the silver school of fish that danced 100 ft (30 m) down along the cliff's edge. My mind made poems of the sight, my ears deafened by the hush of depth, dulled by the pressure of thirty fathoms of ocean. The monochrome landscape, no black, no white, a surreal moonscape of fifty shades of blue, stretched around me, fading into azure mists in all directions. Living dreams of flight, I finned languidly across the gap to the cliff edge, exchanged soaring for swimming, and rejoined the others by the anchor rope. My companions were already beginning their ascent, heading for the first decompression stop 100 ft (30 m) above. I counted disappearing fins, and turned to check there were no stragglers.

Sharks are alien creatures, reminders that the sea is an alien world. They are efficiency come alive, sleek and silent wanderers who belong to the sea in a way man never can. This was my first encounter, a 12 ft (3.6 m) tiger shark that came from nowhere to curve in a wide sweep around the line, cutting in from the deep ocean beyond the drop-off in a circle of curiosity around my pivoting eyes. There's a curious resignation to such a meeting: you know you can't run away to the surface, blood would bubble, you could die. If the shark wants you, you're his, nothing you can do about it. But it's only curious – shark life is boring between meals – and something else large in the sea is a break in the endless swim from one lunch to the next. Sharp black eyes look coldly at me, unblinking, and the tiger stripes run vividly down its back. Tail flicks, and fins jerk, I bore it and its mind wanders to other things as it fades into the mist. I hang there, feeling like bait, my flight crash-landing, and the knowledge of my mortality keenly tapping its fingers on my conscience.

Forty minutes later, breaking surface, Earth feels safe and familiar again.

Eighteen thousand years ago, the cliffs we had swum over, within which Benjamin and Cousteau had explored the Hole in the Wall, a tunnel that led out from the underwater clifftop at 180 ft (54 m) to a cave opening in the edge of the Wall at −240 ft (−72 m), big enough to take one of Cousteau's small submarines, reared high above the sea. Gulls nested where sponges and corals now grow, seals gave birth to cubs in the niches and terraces where the waves cut bays, manatees basked in the warm shallows, made drowsy by early afternoon sun. Where the barrier reef now grows above the cliffs, mangroves, pine forests, high sand dunes once stood. So the world changes. Perhaps, in long years hence, ice will crush the north again and the cliffs will once more echo to the cries of terrestial life, and forget the crunching of coral-grazing fish and the songs of the humpbacks that migrate down the Tongue of the Ocean. But the seals are gone, and the manatees, the crocodiles and iguanas, the giant white owls and many of the other ancient Bahamians. The ghosts of pre-Columbian Arawaks may still paddle their great wooden canoes through the shallow island seas, remembering the tropical paradise that used to be, the great forests of hardwood and pine, the pink rhapsody of vast flamingo flocks, the wild glory of the islands in their youth. The Bahamas are ageing, people raped the wilderness long ago, and only the sea remains, drawing its blue veil over the changes wrought of time. We forget too much.

In 1982, we came back to Conch Sound. A final solo dive the year before by Martyn, while I was in Nassau playing politician with customs officials, had taken him further into the cave than our final joint effort. On our last dive together, just before our limit, he had seen a branching passage high on the right-hand Wall, and had been convinced that this was the real way on. Ignoring the low continuation I had entered, he laid new line down his branch for some distance, in rock-floored and decorated passage, until he came to a roof-fall. Here he stopped, cutting the line, and tying it firmly to one of the fallen boulders. Gaps in the rockfall suggested possible continuations, but on his own, over 2,000 ft (600 m) into the cave and near his air limits, he declined the challenge. It had taken five tanks of air to get him there, three on his person and two stage tanks strapped to a buoyancy compensator and used part-way into the cave. Conch Sound was proving a real challenge, and one of the world's great cave dives. Despite feeling some irritation that Martyn hadn't waited for my return, I was secretly pleased that the cave still cast its gauntlet at our arrogant efforts to reveal its deepest secret.

Now over 2,300 ft (690 m) long, Conch Sound had been explored further than any other submarine cave.

Victoria nosed carefully in to the shallow waters off Deep Creek, following the morning sun in over the Tongue of the Ocean. Warm shafts of light played across the waves, forcing Rob Parker and Julian Walker up in the prow to watch for coral heads, to don their sunglasses and squint through the mirrored dawn. The anchor rattled into water barely deep enough for us to float and we threw ourselves off the deck, to wash away sleep in the cool waters of the bay.

The 1982 expedition was a larger, much more ambitious project, a two-stage effort in which we were hoping both to make a reconnaissance of the South Andros caves and then move back north, to Conch Sound, in pursuit of a record dive beyond the boulder pile at 2,300 ft (690 m). That part of the project would be filmed, and I could already imagine the problems that juggling a couple of dozen people with different aims would offer. It wasn't something I had much experience at. While I sat in contemplation on the upper deck, other eyes were more alert.

'That,' said Clark, our captain, 'was a Hole!'

Less sure, I slipped mask and fins on and went over the side to see.

Across the white, sandy seafloor, a darker patch grew more substantial with every stroke. Soon I was weaving between tall stands of coral, outcrops of elkhorn, brain and staghorn fused together in a small, isolated reef in the shallows of Kemps Bay. They grew so close to the surface that now, at low water, I had to wind my way through a veritable natural maze in this colourful forest of growth to reach the centre.

From the final edge, I almost tumbled down an open shaft, from whose hollow hub the reef spread out in a wide encircling ring. A seemingly bottomless pit yawned beneath my fins, overhung by branching corals and filled with a dancing circus of varicoloured fish. These wove through bright shafts of sun that glanced off ledges many feet below, throwing beams of light across the cavern mouth. The reflections of the waves above pulsed in harmony with the shadows of the cave.

Half an hour later, Julian Walker and I floated 30 ft (9 m) down the shaft, in the last blue rays of sunlight, checking our gauges before heading north into the narrow passage we could just make out, 40 ft (12 m) below. Entering the narrow rift, Julian kept high in the roof, slipping sideways through gaps where the walls closed in, trying to avoid the increased decompression time that would come with the easier route below. Wearing our tanks on our sides, the usual practice in British cave diving, gave us a more streamlined shape for this sort of manoeuvre, but it called for a steady nerve, and careful belaying of the line to ensure it ran through the widest possible bit of the cave. These southern marine caves were different to those further north; the passages were tall and narrow, formed along great fracture lines in the limestone rock. Here, in Coral Hole, the passage dropped to less than 2 ft (0.6 m) wide, and we moved carefully to avoid damaging the wildlife on the walls.

Occasionally, the passage widened into small chambers, and we could look down to what seemed to be a larger passage, thirty and more feet below. We were now at 120 ft (36 m) ourselves, and our route was becoming increasingly haphazard as we searched out the widest gaps in the narrowing roof. This was my first Blue Hole dive with Julian, and I wanted to keep an eye on him – his enthusiasm occasionally needed tempering with a little caution. This seemed far enough for a first dive, and it seemed that we might get further only at a deeper level.

The passage here was beautiful, though. The waters were clear, and the life on the walls could be seen in all its colourful splendour. In the caves, where the only light was our own, the colours came back, and the blues and greens of the outside sea were exchanged for a rainbow profusion of red anemones, yellow and orange sponges, bright corals and crustaceans. Tiny pink and white coral shrimps flickered everywhere in the passage, small puffs of dust-trails marking their wake. Crawfish waved their antennae from crevices, crabs scuttled sideways across walls and floor, too intent on their own business to mind us. Hydroids and delicate crinoids floated gently on the passing outward current, long tentacles trailing in the cool cave outflow. A green light gently filtered down from above as I rose towards the surface.

I looked up, and was captivated by the sight of Julian, outlined against the entrance, framed by the shimmering ripple of wave light and the turquoise silhouette of the elkhorn coral that edged the cave.

As we surfaced near *Victoria*, we saw a small sailboat bobbing at her stern. Curious as to why such a large boat (*Victoria* was all of 40 ft (12 m) – a beautiful wooden trolling boat lent us by the Miami-based Institute for Underwater Archaeology) was anchored so close inshore, Stan and Dorothy Clarke had left their house onshore to see what was going on out in the bay. Quickly deciding that we were completely insane, Stan echoed the general Bahamian interest in Blue Holes, and the general Bahamian reluctance to have anything to do with their inside at all.

'You guys going down those things? You must be crazy. Still, if you think that one's something, you should see the one over there.' Raising anchor, he guided Clark over to another reef a few hundred yards away.

This gaping hole, half the size of a football pitch and over 50 ft (15 m) deep, was again ringed with coral and teeming with life. It resembled nothing more than a gigantic doughnut, a wide ring of reef with a great pit in the centre, a vertical drop some 20–30 ft (6–9 m) to a sloping sandy floor that led down to a narrow opening at the eastern end.

It turned out that all these 'offshore' Holes had their own coral ring, a patch of colourful varied reef on an otherwise sandy plain. Whether the currents kept the rock around the entrances clear enough of sand for corals to anchor and grow, or whether the currents themselves stimulated the coral growth, we don't yet know. Perhaps a mixture of both – the inflowing current certainly pulls much organic material in from a wide area round the cave, making the entrance area and the inner passages a food-rich paradise for the tiny marine animals that live there. The cooler water of the outflow seems to provide some respite for the fish that shelter in the cave mouth. Here, and in the protective branching maze of coral outside, they live in relative safety, screened from predators by the close-knit growth of coral. Here are angelfish, dancing sideways through the branches, multi-hued parrotfish, nibbling noisily at the coral that houses them, slender trumpet fish, tiny pink cardinal-fish, and blue wrasses, and hordes of little territorial sergeant-majors, their yellow-and-black striped bodies earning them the instant sobriquet of 'Dennis-the-Menace' fish. And sometimes great, voluptuous shoals of silversides, moving in shining clouds of syncopated ballet, the ultimate of showmanship in synchronized swimming.

Around the mouths of the caves, schools of grunts and snappers move more steadily between the elkhorn branches, and small groupers lurk in crevice along the outer reef edge. Each cave has its barracuda, slinking in near-invisible stealth in the middle-distance beyond the ring. Buried in the sand on the inshore side, stingrays and the occasional eagle-ray bask in the warm sunlight of the shallow seabed.

Stan and Dorothy took their leave, taking with them Liz Plummer and Anna Sarvary, the female members of our crew, lured ashore by the promise of real beds and showers. Initial grumbles about sexism soon evaporated as, left to our own masculine devices, our unsalubrious evening meal degenerated into obscure but creative rum cocktails on deck under a crescent moon, telling increasingly disreputable stories until the urge to sleep overcame the urge to snigger. We fell asleep watching the undimmed glory of the Milky Way arcing across the sky, to a lullaby of waves.

Dawn, and the approaching drone of Stan's dive boat, woke us in time to greet him. We took a running breakfast, gathering gear and stowing it in the flat-bottomed whaler. The evening before, Stan had excited us with stories of a great Blue Hole on the beach at Mars Bay, locally held to be bottomless.

Onshore, we loaded Stan's small trailer, put those who couldn't fit in his Volkswagen Beetle on top of the gear to hold it down, and headed south. Sitting on the trailer allowed a good, if windy, view of the passing island.

Native houses lined the road in a haphazard ribbon, small, brightly painted, two-or-three room shacks, surrounded by strings of washing and small round-eyed children, who waved shyly back at us as we passed. The dwellings seemed to grow out of the broken, corroded limestone as though idly scattered by some giant child, playing with bright toys. Now and then a gaunt cow, or tribe of goats, cropped unenthusiastically at the surrounding shrubbery, or some motley collection of chickens flew screeching into the bush, scared from the house by an irate mama returning from a long and easy gossip with the neighbours.

Down this end of the island, people made the best part of their living from the sea, men working conch and lobster beds on a seasonal basis, travelling further afield as local beds became worked out. Often away for weeks at a time, following the fishing trail to other islands, or to the sandy cays of the southern banks, they add to their income casually, with some subsistence farming, boating for the occasional tourist, or odd-jobbing, finding work wherever and whenever it comes. Little is hurried, life is on island-time; the rest of the world works differently – that's its problem.

A few add to their income in a darker way. The Bahamas have a long and well-established habit of smuggling; guns and supplies to the Confederacy, liquor during Prohibition, and now harder, more potent drugs, passing through from South America to the streets of the States. Remote beaches and abandoned airstrips are favourite for drug runners flying from Colombia with cargoes of cocaine, breaking up shipments for the fast run by speedboat or light aircraft past the customs boats in the Florida Straits.

Occasionally, overindulging in their own cargo, pilots make a mistake and add their plane to the growing number of wrecks that litter the islands. But profits in this sordid trade are such that one good run will more than pay the price of such a failure. Moral scruples run a poor second to business in this unpleasant and dangerous game.

Passing one such earthstruck flier, its nose wedged irrevocably in the sand, we swung off the main road and tumbled off the trailer on to the beach at Mars Bay.

Sand stretched out from the shore in all directions, low tide turning the bay into a transient desert. On its edge, a gaping, circular Hole fell vertically from in front of our feet to unplumbed, 'bottomless' depths. Before a gathering crowd, and feeling like a couple of colourful court jesters, Rob Parker and I clanked our way from the trailer to the Hole. A silence fell over the watching crowd. Heads were shaken, and bets taken, as we checked our gear. As we could surface from the open shaft with relative ease, and could help each other if equipment malfunctioned, we chose not to wear the full cave diving system, diving instead with a single back-mounted tank and an 'octopus' regulator, each with a spare mouthpiece to share air with the other in emergency.

We sank into a colourless gloom, completely unlike the ocean caves. The walls disappeared as the shaft belled out, and we blew air into our jackets to steady our descent, looking at each other as our only reference in the disorientating dimness of the void. The line wound vertically off our reel as our gauge crept to the 150 ft (45 m) mark. We paused, still floating free in the depths. Rob stayed put, and I continued, dropping to the tip of a sand cone 30 ft (9 m) below. A small shoal of silver fish swam through the beam of my torches as I signalled Rob down. We crept down the dark slope until we reached the limit of our decompression tables, 200 ft (60 m). The slope still dropped away, disappearing into invisible depths, cold and completely dark. Somewhere above, the noonday sun shone, directly over the Hole, back in the world of man.

The chill in our bodies was not entirely due to temperature as we turned and slowly reeled the line back in. The atmosphere of these great *cenotes* is completely different to the clear, warm ocean Holes; an ancient, colourless ambience with a touch of indifference to man. Perhaps the agoraphobic featurelessness of the water, where neither walls nor floor can be seen, where there is nothing to show which way is up save for the rising bubbles of exhausted air, has much to do with it. You are aware that walls enclose you, but you are unable to see them. Where visibility is good, this feeling lessens, but in places like Mars Bay, where visibility is a few metres at best, it is accentuated.

The walls swung back in to view, and we followed them up, past long globular sponges and brown algal growths that did little to make the place more friendly. Our audience looked surprised to see us return from the deeps. We smiled at them, and made our escape.

Dorothy fed us on grits, bacon and coffee as we relaxed after the dive. The Clarkes had life well sorted; coming to Andros years before, they had fallen in love with the place and eventually made it their home. Their house they built themselves, powering it by the sun and wind. Stan himself made the solar panels and windmill on the roof; water came from rain-catchment, Dorothy's productive garden, an example to the locals, was irrigated from a well. If a little out of touch with some aspects of the outside world ('Reggae? Who's he?'), their lifestyle had a simple meaning that I for one envied.

The sun set as we sailed north, towards the next stage of the expedition. The rest of the team was flying out to meet us at Conch Sound. Gypsy lights on the shore slipped by as the others slept. Alone on watch, I listened as Al Stewart sang of island goodbyes:

> . . . it's time to haul the anchor up, and leave the land astern.
> We'll be gone before the dawn returns, like voices on the wind . . .

As night grew towards morning, I lay awake, a strange depression growing. I could imagine the multitude of problems that would soon sweep in as we became land-based and grew in numbers. The filming of the next stage was due to provide a fair amount of bother, and I suspected that the organization of the north island stage wouldn't be at all easy.

Perhaps it is only with small groups that a real sense of involvement in a project like this is felt? We were moving into a more complex environment, with changing pressures, and I wondered how, after the relaxed days in the south, we were going to cope with the change.

Nicolls Town presents its best side to the sea. Coconut palms fringe the beach, adding a touch of traditional Caribbean, and sheltering the settlement from the elements. Behind the palms, the township sprawls out in a chequered grid, the northernmost and one of the largest of the Andros communities. It boasts several shops, a modern supermarket and petrol station, and a comfortable hotel, with an associated villa complex nearby. Traditional wooden shacks are scattered in cheerful disorder, surrounded by flowering shrubs and fruit trees, a curious juxtaposition of old and new, incongruously trimmed by the large American cars and powerful speedboats that lie outside certain homesteads.

Back in the UK, the Bahamas Tourist Authority had arranged for us to use two of the villas in the 'Tradewind' complex as our base. Summer in the Bahamas is 'off-season', and many of the villas were empty. Living in tents or rough accommodation, and doing the type of diving we intended to in Conch Sound, would give us no respite from the 'no-see-ums', the mosquitoes and the occasional tropical storm. As much as any front-line sportsmen, we needed to be fit and healthy, to have somewhere to keep our equipment safe, to repair it and us, to keep things as free as possible from the insidious grains of sand that crept in everywhere. Six, and later ten, in a four-berth villa wasn't quite the lap of luxury, but it was better than many of the alternatives.

Liz and Anna got to grips with the organization of food and supplies, and while the others dealt with the air compressor, filling tanks, I tried to tackle the transport problem. It soon became obvious that the trucks we'd been promised by department heads in Nassau would not be forthcoming, and we desperately needed a vehicle to move us and our equipment the two miles or so to Conch Sound each day. The Tradewind truck, a beaten-up old pickup used to shift rubbish once a week was begged as a make-do, though with its distinctive lack of serious braking ability, and doors that resented closure, it wasn't quite what we'd hoped for. Later, the problem was resolved by the local 'mayor', Harry Treco, who arranged for the town refuse truck to run us further afield when required. This was altogether a larger and more salubrious conveyance, despite the cockroach colony beneath the floor, and the occasionally indelicate aroma when the day's diving followed the week's refuse collection.

While we were overcoming the small problem of settling in to a new base, Duncan Gibbins and the rest of the film crew joined us, moving into the second villa, and adding their pile of camera and sound equipment to the transport nightmare.

The great entrance collapse of Conch Sound Blue Hole lies only a few score yards from the shore, in the middle of a shallow bed of eel-grass. Old conch shells litter the beach, a memorial to generations of fishermen who made a living from the shell beds that gave the bay its name. From the beach it was possible to wade the short distance to the edge of the Hole, and stand waist-deep on the edge of the drop.

The road to the Sound finishes almost on the beach; a great asset, for our equipment could be driven to the water's edge. That evening, we donned masks and fins and swam out though the warm shallows to the Blue Hole. Tide tables had indicated that the current would still be flowing strongly into the cave. This wasn't the best time to visit – the shallowness of the bay and the great amount of organic material in suspension in the water meant that it was thick with debris, all being swept into the cave. Visibility was down to 20 ft (6 m) or so, and the newcomers to the cave could get little idea of the size and complexity of the entrance area.

Five openings joined together in a great arc over a hundred feet across, descending over ledges and boulders for over 70 ft (20 m) to a twilight zone on the edge of darkness. Tiny fin worms, waving hydroids and shy anemones covered the rocks, and great schools of parrotfish and snapper cruised effortlessly around the boulders. Through these swam a bewildering variety of smaller fish, nosing each other in defence of tiny squares of territory, or chasing around in endless games of follow-my-leader through the clefts and shadows of the jumbled chaos of the entrance.

Two hours later, Rob, Julian and I entered the cave to replace the line removed from the entrance passages the year before, to discourage casual intruders. The small sunken launch still lay jammed among boulders 10 ft (3 m) down, and this again became our underwater base. The orange line was tied to its side and we floated down, exchanging the last of the twilight for the darkness of the cave. The currents had just changed, and we swam into a mounting outflow. Last year's yellow line soon appeared, fringed by a 1 in (2.54 cm)-long growth of tiny hydroids, but otherwise unaffected by a year's immersion in the submarine currents. We joined the line together, making one continuous line (we hoped) from the boat to the boulder choke at the end of the cave. We pressed on in, pulling ourselves along the floor as far as the first stalagmite chamber, over 300 ft (90 m) into the cave.

For Rob Parker and Julian, it was their first experience of diving against such a strong Blue Hole current, and they found it quite an eye-opener. The swim in was in constant battle, even with our buoyancy vests empty and the journey made by hauling ourselves along the rough coral floor. In the chamber, reaching our air margins, we turned round with relief and were swept out so quickly that we were bounced off rock pillars, scraped along walls, and generally tossed around the passage before the current spent its force in the wide entrance area.

I surfaced with a splitting headache; an accident earlier in the day with a falling back-pack had left a deep gash in my forehead, and the pressure rubbing from my mask hurt considerably. I'd tried side-mounting two of our large 105 cu. ft (9 cu. m) tanks as well, and had made ponderous progress with such a heavy and unwieldy system. Longer dives would need a lighter or more balanced rig.

So, for the next dive, the system that became standard for long penetrations was adopted. Two 80 cu. ft (6.8 cu. m) tanks were worn, one on each side on a specially designed harness, and a 105 cu. ft (9 cu. m) tank was carried on our backs. On dry land, this all weighed about 100 lb (45 kg), and was only really manageable underwater, where the increased buoyancy dropped the weight to about an equivalent 10 lb (4.5 kg). It was still pretty bulky, and not very streamlined, so progress up the cave was of necessity slow and deliberate. Using the currents, riding the last of the inflow into the cave and returning on the growing outflow, would make things easier, but the change-overs were not entirely predictable, varying by as much as 40 minutes from their predicted time each cycle. We would simply have to make the best of whatever conditions we found on the day.

The lines to the end had to be checked, and one of the two possible ways on chosen for our explorations. Strewn across the sand, our diving equipment made a bright sight in the early morning sun. We each had wetsuits of different colours for easy underwater identification and this, coupled with the yellows, blacks and reds of the rest of the gear, lent us an air as colourful as any of the harlequin fish that circled us in the entrance.

Rob and Julian each wore three 80s and both carried an extra 105 in their hands as staging tanks for my swim to the end. We missed the change-over again, entering against the growing outward current. For the other two, under the added burden of the stage tanks, it was a struggle. Julian later wrote in his diary:

The visibility was poor, stirred up by the two divers in front. I was using a lot of air, bottom-walking along with two hands on the tank, and had to stop to catch my breath every five or ten minutes. I worked my way steadily through my tanks, onto my third full one. We passed through Stalagmite Chamber, and on to the 850 ft [225 m] mark. Here Rob (Palmer) had used all but 50 bars from his back-mounted 105, so we swopped this for Rob Parker's full stage one. Mine, I left tied to the line for his return.

This simple précis hid a lot of effort on Rob and Julian's part. Their large tanks proved a real hindrance, and both used air quickly, hauling themselves from rock to rock in the strong current. Free swimming was impossible, progress was reduced to a horizontal, underwater stumble, pushing and pulling along the bottom, with an occasional desperate tug on the thick line. Even without a hand-held tank I found it heavy going, and was grateful for the occasional pause as they caught up.

In the chamber, things got a little easier as the current dispersed in the wide passage. We pushed off walls and huge, old corroded columns festooned with weed and sponge until 850 ft (250 m) in, we came to a small hollow surrounded by solid formations. Here, sheltered a little from the flow, I struggled out of my back harness and exchanged it for the fresh 105. I watched them disappear back towards the entrance, carried slowly away on the current with the empty tank between them.

With three full tanks, I turned back to the cave, and carried on alone down the line. A year back in England, analysing my feelings about this remote passage, had changed my outlook . . . I felt less in awe of it, less apprehensive about what the next corner might bring. Caution was tinged with a growing anticipation as I tried to slow my breathing and conserve as much air as possible before I reached new passages.

The stalagmite caverns gave way to the long rolling dunes of sand that I remembered from the year before, their featureless surface broken every now and then by small stalagmite islands. These emerged dimly from the gloom in front, and faded slowly into the sand-cloud of my passing. Island-hopping in this fashion, I came at last to the junction where Martyn's line curved up and over to the right, leading into a part of the cave unknown to me. I swam past it, wanting to check the original end first, and shortly reached the knot that fixed the end of the line to the cave wall. This was it, everything beyond was new and unexplored. Once again, the extra spurt of adrenalin increased my heartbeat.

Disappointment. Within a few yards, the roof swung down and the passage became low and wide, less than 3 ft (0.9 m) high. Still with a current in my face, I pushed on between rock pendants hanging from the lowering roof until my chest was forced into the silt and my tanks scraped the roof. Everything looked brown and uninviting, and my view of the cave was suddenly obliterated as a fine cloud of sediment swirled and blinded me. The tank on my back snagged at the roof as I struggled to turn around, pushing me further into the mud. By touch, I trapped the floating coils of line, winding them back on the reel, and groped my way back to the knot. Martyn's passage seemed suddenly much more inviting.

As soon as I turned into it I felt, as he had, that this was the way on. Rising over the small ledge that marked its beginning, I came into a rock-floored passage about 6 ft (1.8 m) high that grew larger as I followed the old line along. The walls again played host to tiny sponges and crabs, smaller than before, and a lonely crawfish darted backwards under a boulder, disturbed by the unwelcome glare of my lights. Soon I reached the jumbled collapse of boulders that marked Martyn's limit, 2,300 ft (690 m) into the cave. It seemed to present a formidable barrier to further progress. Tying my line on a little before the pile, I swam across the choke, seeking the best possible way through. There were only two possibilities, a narrow rift on the east side, and an awkward and constricted squeeze between two boulders close to Martyn's final knot. These were the size of small trucks, it was a committing move.

By now I was right on my air limit, too little left to attempt such a squeeze. I left the reel behind a rock, out of the current, and turned for the distant entrance. The dive had already lasted over an hour, and the passages here were close to 90 ft (27 m) deep. I already needed to decompress before surfacing, and the time for this was increasing with each minute spent in the cave.

But the current was with me and the outward swim was fast. A little over half-an-hour after dropping the reel I was back in the sunken boat, 10 ft (3 m) below the surface. But even the bright bustle of the entrance palled as the minutes ticked by. My head still ached, and even the hot Bahamian sun overhead could not fully penetrate the water; thermal conduction was drawing my body heat slowly away into the sea. Three hours after the dive began it came as a real relief to rise the last few feet to the surface and swim across the eel-grass to the shore.

We decided that further dives should wait for Martyn and the rest of the team, due to join us in a couple of days. We spent the next day visiting Dick and Rosie Birch at Small Hope Bay, old friends of George Benjamin. Leaning on the bar of his dive centre, Dick told us why George had been able both to build up a successful business in Toronto and spend so much time on Andros. He appointed a manager, who asked him what he should do if anything went wrong while George was away exploring.

'Easy,' said George. 'Ring me on Andros, and I'll fly back straight away. First thing I'll do is fire you, then I'll fix the problem.' George's business went from strength to strength.

While we waited, the film crew seized the opportunity to visit the Turks and Caicos Islands to interview Jaques Mayol. Mayol, who held the world record for deep-diving on a single lungful of air, was out there training for another attempt. He uses a series of yoga-related exercises to relax mind and body before taking hold of a specially designed weight on the end of a guiderope. Then he breathes in, and goes for it. At the time, he had managed to reach the phenomenal depth of 300 ft (90 m), returning to the surface in a self-induced semi-coma.

He is also fairly commercially minded about the whole thing. Before the interview he dropped heavy hints about a fee. Duncan, our director, blanched a little and asked him what sort of figure he had been thinking about.

'Bear in mind,' said Mayol, 'that a large American film company recently paid me $3,000 for a five-minute interview, and translate that into your own resources.'

'That's easy,' beamed Duncan in relief. 'In that case, you owe us about £10.'

Back in Nicolls Town, the enforced idleness was beginning to strain tempers. The long wait for action, coupled with continuing problems with transport and compressors, was creating a rather tense atmosphere, not helped much by the individuality of the other members. Cave divers tend to have strong personalities and working as a team can be difficult when not actually in the water. Rob and Julian hated the inactivity with all the fervour of youth, having come to Andros to explore underwater caves, not to cope with the trials of expedition logistics. Being as much of an individual as the others, I was reluctant to delegate, and found myself getting involved with the problems without noticing the effect they were having on the other members of the team. Spirits were at a low when the final members of the expedition arrived.

Nor did they improve. Martyn arrived in a black mood, having fallen foul of the Bahamian transport system, most of his diving gear having been flown in error to another island. The day became a tense and difficult one, with one person after another giving vent to their frustrations, and me getting more and more irritable as a result. We seemed completely unable to communicate with each other, a problem that was as much my fault as theirs.

I had developed to an unfortunate degree the irritating habit of refusing to accept that I might be wrong without arguing each point through to a conclusion and being convinced one way or the other. Martyn was upset about the film, which he had been against from the start, afraid that it might interfere too much with his diving, and was unwilling to accept the financial necessity of its involvement. Without it, we simply wouldn't be there. Our arguments grew petty, and we had little to do with each other for the rest of the day.

But now that the full team was in the field, things began to move more swiftly. One team, under the guidance of Ken and Laurie Jones, moved to Forfar and began a scientific examination of the forest Holes in the interior. At Nicolls Town, we set a current meter in Conch Sound Hole to record the tidal changes more accurately, and began filming in the entrance area. The divers checked their gear out in smaller Blue Holes nearby, and we began to get acclimatized for the attempts on the end of Conch Sound.

The first dive saw Martyn and I together at the 'terminal' boulder choke.

Despite the latent aggression above water, our teamwork underwater was excellent, born of long experience together. Communication was almost telepathic, a small movement of a hand, a shrug, a look. There was an unspoken agreement that Martyn should have first go at the choke, and I hung back while he removed his back-mounted tank and wriggled through successfully with side-mounts alone. The sounds of his passing faded, and I was left alone.

After a few minutes, I became bored. I looked at the squeeze, and decided that I might be able to make it through with the backpack on. This would be worth trying: long dives beyond the choke would need such a configuration of tanks. It took a couple of attempts, and some air, but I soon found myself clear of the constriction and into big passage again. Martyn's line snaked off into the distance, and I followed it, catching him up at about 2,600 ft (780 m). As the roll of line on the reel grew smaller, I turned and made my way back to the squeeze, leaving Martyn to unwind the last 100 ft (30 m) or so and follow me through once I'd cleared it. While I waited, back in the main cave, I sorted out a large tangle of loose line that had come adrift from the wall, bundling it into a ball, and tying it off at the end.

The dive out was exhilarating. We reached our stage tanks, and straddled them, riding them like scooters down the entrance tunnels in the full force of the outflow.

It was raining outside. Tiny craters pocked the surface above us, vanishing in instantaneous creation as we decompressed.

The next attempt fell to Martyn, while I spent the day with the film crew. The end of the cave grew further from the entrance, each dive now becoming technically a world record in submarine cave exploration. The furthest point grew to 3,100 ft (930 m). Martyn had been side-tracked into a blind bedding tunnel at the end point of our joint dive, but had discovered the main way on again after branching off a little way back down the line. The new end was a narrow rift, the cave had turned through 90° and the way on lay through this constricted vertical crack, over 3,000 ft (900 m) from daylight and 100 ft (30 m) below the bay.

The problems of remote location diving on a low budget were making themselves too apparent. Compressors broke down, transport was irregular, petrol supplies would run out . . . tempers would fray in return. The nearest spare parts were in Miami, and at this point we flew one of the film crew over to buy enough spares to repair our equipment, a two-day trip that left us with little to do but disagree and make short trips inland with what air we could muster.

Duncan had quickly caught on to the undercurrent of aggression between Martyn and I, and was trying to bring this out in the film. On the morning of my planned attempt on the end, he interviewed me in front of the camera on the beach, and asked a number of pointed questions, which I answered honestly, avoiding any blatant reference to the ill-feeling, but admitting to the difficulties of working with many well-developed egos, including my

Bahamian cave diving is thirsty work. Martyn Farr cools off with a quick drink after struggling into his gear before a photographic dive in Conch Sound. *(Photo: Rob Palmer)*

own. I mentioned this to Martyn, due to be interviewed next, and found him as unhappy as I was about any question of airing our disagreements in public. I suggested he listen to the tape if he was really concerned, but Duncan, quite understandably for him, wanted to do his interview with Martyn before this, in case my answers clouded Martyn's opinion. Habitually, things blew out of all proportion, and Martyn got into such a state that he refused to dive until he'd listened to the tape, proclaiming that if he didn't hear it, he wouldn't dive again. By now, heartily sick of such pettiness, I told Duncan to play it to him, and cancelled the day's dive. I had no intention of going into the water with one of the people I was relying on to support me acting in such a way. There was too much tension in the air for safety. There was nothing on the tape of real note, and I suspect Martyn found it very anti-climactic. It was several days before the tides were suitable for another Conch Sound push.

The day started early, just before dawn. There was a brief aggressive exchange with Martyn during breakfast, and I came close to lashing out, keeping my anger in check by some unknown reserve. Tempers simmered, and cooled. We drove to the Hole at 7.30am, with the morning sun still low on the horizon, and had a leisurely kitting-up session on the beach. Martyn disappeared with Rob Parker, to deposit stage tanks for me at 2,300 ft (690 m) and 1,600 ft (480 m) respectively. I dived at 8.55, breathing off a hand-held tank to 1,600 ft (480 m). Tony Boycott, our doctor, swam with me, picking up a stage tank deposited the day before at 900 ft (270 m), and taking it on to 1,500 ft (450 m), where he tied it to the line for my return. I left my part-used 80 at 1,600 ft (480 m), exchanging it for the full one left by Rob minutes before. Just before the squeeze at 2,300 ft (690 m), I changed this for the one Martyn had just deposited, and passed the constriction with four full tanks.

In the large cave at the far side of the boulders, I almost wept with frustration. My full line reel, fastened loosely to my belt, had disappeared somewhere in the last few hundred feet of cave, before the choke. I could not venture safely into any unexplored passage without a line, and it looked, after all the traumas of the past few days, like the dive was a waste of time. I decided that the least I could do would be to take the full stage tank as far into the cave as possible, and leave it there for Martyn's next attempt. Then I remembered that Martyn had left a part-full reel in the blind side passage 200 ft (60 m) or so ahead. If I could get in the passage with my back-mounted tank and reach the reel, I could rewind it as far as the main line and then have at least a 200 ft (60 m) of line to explore with.

Leaving the stage tank at the line junction, I pushed my way up the side tunnel, my 105 scraping the roof, and the confined struggle raising silt from the walls and floor in clouds. I reached the reel, and turned with difficulty, winding the line awkwardly back on the spool, and using too much air doing so. I was panting by the time I regained the stage tank, and hung there, catching my breath, until my pulse dropped far enough to continue calmly.

Moving on, I came to a region where the floor was riddled with deep holes, dropping to some unseen lower series of passages. Beyond this lay Martyn's rift, a narrow canyon about 3 ft (0.9 m) wide, awkward and constricted to pass. I clipped the part-used stage tank to Martyn's final knot and tied my own short reel on. Straying slightly higher than the earlier line, I found the rift easier to pass than it looked. Twenty feet (6 m) or so of the narrow canyon brought me again to an open passage, about 30 ft (9 m) wide and 6 ft (1.8 m) high, and I swam free. But all too soon an unwelcome tug on the reel told me that I was finished. I stared down the large, open cave into the unexplored darkness, and cursed. The urge to abandon the line and swim that bit further was desperate. I moved a few feet more, but sanity kept hold. The entrance was now a full kilometre away, 3,300 ft (1,000 m).

I tied the cord to the wall, and, as a lighthearted touch, left a small Union Jack fluttering from it in the current. Duncan had passed this to me just before the dive, with a tongue-in-cheek comment about our 'underwater Everest'. I shot a few feet of film from my helmet-mounted 8 mm camera, and turned for home.

Back in the rift, the reduced visibility gave me a nightmare moment as stage tank, line reel and gauges all became entangled at the narrowest point. Again, precious air was spent sorting out the mess, I felt acutely aware of just how far from safety I actually was. After that, the boulder choke constriction came as a bit of an anti-climax, gravity's aid making it easier going back than coming up. I recovered the second of the stage tanks and made my way down the cave, aided now by the current, and feeling rather like an overdressed Christmas tree with five tanks, line reel and the plethora of valves and gauges that festooned my suit.

Julian and I arrived almost simultaneously at 1,600 ft (480 m) from opposite directions. I passed him one empty tank, then, as we reached Tony's stage cylinder, the other. The rest of the trip out was uneventful, seven league strides down the final few hundred feet as the current really took us, depositing us in dappled sunlight below the entrance.

Decompression today was a novel experience, underwater cameraman Pete Scoones had rigged up a small transducer microphone as an underwater speaker, and connected it to a Walkman on the surface. A slate came down, 'Tell us when you want to boogie', scrawled across it. I stuck the little bone-conductor speaker beneath my helmet and got an instant blast of Al Stewart.

Four and a half hours after entering the water, I rose to a reception committee of film crew feet by the Hole's edge. As I broke surface, a cry of 'Shit, total camera malfunction' rent the air. Bang went my chance of fame!

We had time for one more concerted push at the end, this time the turn once again being Martyn's. Two days later we began staging tanks into the cave, and setting generator-powered lights into the stalagmite chamber. Martyn, who had again swum in to stage a tank before the choke, came out looking rather subdued.

It transpired that he had staged the tank successfully, but when he paused to change his regulators, moving on to his last full tank, the mouthpiece had resolutely failed to provide air. Nothing he could do could persuade it to work, so he had turned for home, aware that now he had much less than his full reserve supply of air. Moving quickly back down the cave, concentrating more on getting out than on his surroundings, he had become entangled in the line about 1,600 ft (480 m) in. Unable to reach behind to free the knot from his backpack, he'd had to draw his knife and cut the line to free himself. By the time he reached Rob Parker and his inward stage tank in Stalagmite Chamber, he was close to nervous exhaustion, very aware of the thin dividing line between existence and death.

But he recovered quickly, and was ready the next day for the attempt on the end. His urge to be in front submerged all else, too bluntly at times, but there was no doubting his commitment to the exploration of the cave. Julian swum in that night to reconnect the lines, and the compressor ran late, pumping the thirty-odd tanks needed for the following day.

Tony Boycott, our doctor, and I dived first, with two stage tanks for the 1,600 ft (480 m) mark, one for the outward journey, one for Martyn's continued inward swim. We overshot slightly, looking for a belay point that had been lost during Martyn's epic the day before. Taken in on the current, our sense of time was affected, and we arrived at the junction at 1,850 ft (555 m) before we realized. Tony left his tank there, but I swam back down the cave, looking for Martyn, who by now must have been getting well down his first stage tank. We met at 1,700 ft (510 m), and I took his empty tank in exchange for the fresh one. With a small wave, Martyn went on, disappearing into the gloom.

As we left the cave, Rob and Julian entered it, Rob swimming to 1,500 ft (450 m), and Julian moving even further in, to the choke at 2,300 ft (690 m). There they began a lonely wait for Martyn's return.

By this time, Martyn had reached the end of my line, and attached his new reel. Moving down the passage into new cave, he was astounded when the walls suddenly disappeared out of sight and he found himself hanging in the centre of a great void, an immense underground chamber, utterly different to anything we had so far seen. Here, so far from the entrance, the stalagmites were clean and crystalline, free of the organic corrosion that marked those further back down the cave. A small film of dust was all that hid their crystal sheen; the only life a few solitary ascidians that hung flaccidly on a rock.

He swam on, from stalagmite to stalagmite, into an area devoid of all life. Eventually, a wall came into view, and he followed it towards a cloud of murky water ahead. There, in the mists, lay a thick guideline – his own. He had somehow swum full circle without realizing it.

With plenty of air to spare, he turned and followed the wall in the other direction. Soon, small life-forms began to appear again, simple sponges and sea-squirts that hung delicately from beneath small outcrops, straining to filter what little food remained in the currents that reached this far in. This suggested that a way on lay near here, and through the boulders that floored the cave Martyn could see black holes. Their depth lay beyond the scope of this dive.

Here, at the end of nowhere, Martyn came across a solitary swimmer, one of the pale blind cave fish, *Lucifuga,* hanging in solitary confinement in the dark waters of the chamber, utterly indifferent to the presence of this brash intruder. Martyn turned, and left it to its silent domain.

The trail of bubbles leading from the entrance told us Martyn was returning, 2¾ hours after he had disappeared. But it was a further 3¼ hours before he could surface, 3¼ hours of lying underwater, purging the nitrogen from his tissues before he could safely breathe air without a mouthpiece, looking at the sunlight only a few feet away. Rob Parker greeted him with a bottle of cold beer as he broke surface, and grinned with success. Martyn had reached a point 3,800 ft (1,140 m) into a Blue Hole, the longest dive anyone had ever made in these astonishing, delightful sub-marine caves.

CHAPTER SEVEN

Stargate, Elvenhome and the Ocean Holes

*A*FTER THE 1982 expedition, it was interesting to play the analyst and examine the many things that had gone wrong. Despite the heartaches and unpleasantness, the organization of such an ambitious project had been interesting, approached on my part with fascination – but with little attention to detail. I needed someone close by to help with the finer points of administration, which I tended to find rather a bore, and to nag me into action when I let minutiae slide. There hadn't really been anyone with sufficient time or motivation to do that – I had found Martyn, as deputy-leader, more concerned with the physical exploration of the caves, and too unsympathetic to the concept of science and film, to have made that sort of delegation easy. It seemed as though I couldn't get my opinions across in the field without being, or seeming, aggressive or offensive. I felt I wasn't much good at organizing large groups of individuals whose self-motivation should have allowed them to organize themselves *in situ*. But they had looked too much to me, and I felt that I had somehow let them down.

We had really been three expedition teams, and the central one, of exploration, had been egotistically reluctant to involve itself fully with the others, the filming and scientific ones. My personal disgust at this attitude didn't help either, nor did my inexperience at dealing with such problems. It was a salutary education. I talked to many other experienced expeditionaries – mountaineers, cavers, polar explorers and others – and found that I wasn't alone in my somewhat disastrous position. Leadership is inherently a thankless and pilloried employment. It made me feel a little better. The project had been a success, materially if not socially, and who could say which was the more important?

The next summer, Rob Parker, Julian and I worked in the Blue Holes of eastern Grand Bahama, the three of us finding that small is indeed beautiful, generally enjoying ourselves more, and discovering thousands of feet of new caves. My disagreements with Martyn had left me disillusioned about his abilities as part of a team – he needed too much to be in the number one position – and I had no real interest in working further along those lines. I suppose in many ways this was a shame, we'd certainly made an effective team, but the division was too deep. As time went on, and we explored more of the underwater, underground Bahamas, I learned a lot more about how to (and so how not to) go about things in the field.

It was much against my better judgement, therefore, that I found myself back in the Bahamas in 1985 with Operation Raleigh, a large international round-the-world expedition led by the ubiquitous John Blashford-Snell. Many of my friends, who had encountered Blashford-Snell and his unique approach to exploration before, had warned me not to get involved with the operation, and its pseudo-military background did make me somewhat cautious.

But the concept had appealed, the bringing together of young people from many parts of the world in an expedition setting, and I set aside my reservations to help co-ordinate the projects for the first phase of the Operation, a three-month mini-expedition to several of the Bahamian islands.

As the field dates drew closer, my worries became greater. The organization in London seemed to be filled with pretty young Sloanes and clean-cut military types, most of whom had less idea than I'd had in 1981 of the problems such a large civilian expedition would hit in the field. One or two of the pivotal people, like Roger Chapman (a man for whom I have a tremendous admiration), appeared to be working themselves virtually to the bone to hold the whole thing together. A few months before the Operation got under way, my fears were confirmed. Returning from a reconnaissance to Grand Bahama with Alan Westcob, the leader of the phase and then a major in the Army, we sat in John Blashford-Snell's London flat and discussed the problems we saw lying ahead. To me, one of the biggest was that of the attitude within Raleigh's command structure. The whole thing had more than the essence of a military operation, and this would go down like a ton of bricks in the Bahamas, still a relatively new self-governing country within the Commonwealth. I pleaded with John to tone it down, and got the abrupt response.

'You must realize, Rob, that I am paid by the Army to publicize the Army. That is what Operation Raleigh is largely about.'

So, fine – at least it was out in the open. I thought about withdrawing, and probably should have, but felt that I had committed myself beyond the point of being easily able to do so.

We had negotiated the use of a marina on Cat Island with its cautious owner and by the time I had watched Blashford-Snell roar into it, setting several expensive boats rocking hard against their moorings with the wake from the twin-outboard Avon Searider he insisted on treating as his personal craft, and shouting 'The British are here' through a loudhailer and then roaring out again, I was pretty sick of the whole affair. The owner looked at this peculiar figure, standing in the boat fully kitted out for jungle warfare, and then at us.

'If that ***** lands on my marina, I'm gonna tie him to a tree and let the ants get him.' He stalked off. Blashford-Snell didn't bother to come ashore and thank him for the use of his marina, but he did proceed to leave us with only three-quarters of our supplies, night having fallen while we waited for him to stop playing explorer and organize the landing of the gear. It sort of set the scene for the entire trip, the struggle of scientific and directing staff against the pseudo-military mind, of people who were aware and could understand the unexpected and unusual events that dominate field expeditions, and those who needed everything compartmentalized into neat orders and endless lists, and who led from behind. We grew to suspect that many of the military personnel in the command structure had been released from their posts for the duration for other than altruistic reasons. That the 'venturers', the young men and women who had raised hundreds of pounds to come on the expedition got any adventure at all was often due to directing staff simply bending or ignoring 'rules' to make sure they did. Bits of Raleigh were pleasant, and there were many happy moments, usually when the flagship, the *Sir Walter Raleigh* and its military command team were elsewhere.

But the Blue Holes project was anything but successful. Denied the transport we needed both at land and sea to get to the Holes on a regular basis, we fell back largely on cataloguing different sites, and concentrating effort at a very few. One of these was a spectacular opening beneath a small cliff, found by a Canadian girl, Jenny Shaw, on a wander through the forest along a huge fault line that ran parallel to the coast of South Andros. Poor Jenny had a major encounter with poisonwood soon after, and missed out on the early exploration of the Hole. Poisonwood is one of the nastier tricks the Bahamian jungle plays on people – some are immune, others have the most appalling histamine reactions imaginable just by standing underneath it. Jenny verged on the latter – within a day or so she was virtually blind, and in excruciating agony. It took a week or so for her to return to normal, by which time we'd discovered that the cave, which we called Stargate, was one of the most stunning underwater caves we had seen.

The entrance was overhung by a rock roof, sheltering it from the worst of the weather, and from much of the organic debris that fell into the other inland holes. It was this organic input, and direct sunlight, that was responsible for the sulphurous bacterial layers that lay near the surface, and around the mixing zone, of most of the inland holes. Stargate's sheltered entrance meant that the surface waters were unusually clear, and cooler than those of the other nearby caves.

The first two into the Hole, Gary Hardington and Pete Hatt, diving for initial water samples, came up bubbling with excitement. By this time I was in the water with another cave diver, Bob Hartlebury, and this enthusiasm

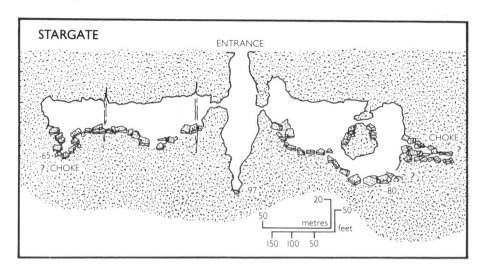

became infectious. Sinking into the depths, we realized why Gary and Pete had been so awestruck. The walls were visible all the way to the mixing zone, and the clarity of the water was amazing. It was like falling down an immense well, skydiving through clear green waters into nightfall.

Passing into the mixing zone, 40 ft (12 m) down, was like falling through clouds. Vision blurred, and Bob became a vague outline a few feet away. Instant myopia. Bob was unused to this, and moved closer. A few feet more, and we were out of it, emerging from the clouds into a chasm of awesome clarity, and stunning dimensions. The walls went up, and down, and out to either side as far as we could see. Floating in mid-water, at a depth approaching 120 ft (36 m), we hung in dreamlike suspension, looking down an endless tunnel, unable to move. Normally, in dreams, this might be accompanied by a sensation of unease, or outright fear, the ingredients of nightmare. The feeling here was completely different; one of awe, of immensity, of staggering delight.

The walls below the mixing zone were white, clear of the organic film that darkened those at shallower depths, and which absorbed much of the filtering sunlight. Here, the rock reflected light, and gave the curious impression that, as we left the mixing zone, the cave actually became brighter.

Bob and I swam north, tying on a guideline as we left daylight, and entered a giant passage, an upside-down canyon with a roof and no floor. The walls were draped with clean white flowstone, sometimes covering the rock with a shining coat of crystal, sometimes gathering into forms; slim stalactites or thin, translucent curtains that folded in graceful curves down to a sharp calcite point. Tiny white specks moved through the clear water, and close examination revealed these to be microscopic crustaceans, minute animals that had evolved over millennia to live in the total darkness of the caves. We had seen these occasionally on other islands, but rarely in such profusion. The cave went on, and we moved slowly in the immense canyon.

At length, the walls closed in ahead, and distant rocks rose from an invisible floor to signal the end. We tied the line to the final wall and cut the reel free.

Motioning to Bob to wait at the belay, I sank further into the depths to see if the cave continued lower down. At -135 ft (-40 m), the walls changed colour, quite suddenly, from clean white rock to a dusky grey. Fine brown silt lay on ledges and the passage at depth had a more oppressive air. Something higher up, perhaps a current flow, kept the cave clean. Here it seemed stagnant and less attractive. By now I could see a mass of broken boulders below and no easy way on through their chaotic design. I rejoined Bob and we swam out, slightly stunned by the immensity of our discovery.

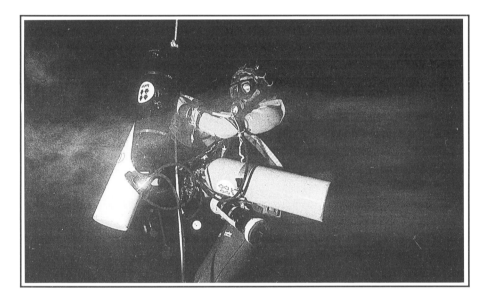

Decompressing in the mists of the mixing zone after a dive to the end of Stargate's South Passage. *(Photo: Rob Palmer)*

The south passage was the same, a huge canyon that ran in a straight line for 400 ft (120 m) to an apparent rock wall. Leaving Bob there, I went alone down on the right hand side, where at a depth of 125 ft (37.5 m), a small gap led through the wall to another cavern. Huge blocks sat poised in the roof, waiting to fall on an unsuspecting diver and there was no sign of a floor below, altogether a dramatic sight.

Later, I made a short dive in the main south passage before the gap to try and find the elusive floor. Leaving Bob and our marine biologist, Mary Stafford Smith, floating at -120 ft (-36 m), I clipped a line to the main one and sank down into the chasm. The boundary between the clean white cave and the brown came and went, and I was sure I could taste a faint sulphur tang. The silt on the walls grew subtly thicker, and as I sank towards the -200 ft (-60 m) mark I could make out large boulders jammed across the cave below. They seemed to block the cave entirely, and I could see no way forward. Here, there was no real narrowing of the cave walls, and I wondered just how thick and secure the blockage was.

Tests we made on the water showed that the deeper cave, below the mixing zone, was as saline as the sea. The shallower waters were not fresh, but brackish, and in nearby caves we could detect a definite current flowing along the line of the fracture. The great fault was acting as an underground tidal 'river', channelling the flow along a potentially great cave parallel to the coast. Whether the passages were open all the way, or the flow occasionally broke up into fissures too small for man to pass, was beyond us. To the south, we could trace the fault along a chain of surface openings, some of which led into small caves, most of which were choked at shallow depths. It ran along the shoreline just north of the small settlement of Smith's Hill, and left the land where a series of small Blue Holes split the shallows just below the low tide mark. Beyond this, we could see from the air that it led to caves we'd explored in 1982, to Coral Hole, to Giant Doughnut, and to other blue openings surrounded by coral reefs that we had yet to visit.

To the north, the trail of the fault meandered a little, a few degrees either side of compass North. It skirted the shore just north of the Bluff, the largest of the South Andros settlements, then turned further inland where the coast bulged out, running through thick forests of broad-leaved tropical bush to the tip of the island. There it broke the creek bank in a wide blue lake, and a line of yellow sand aimed straight at Benjamin's Blue Holes in the South Bight. The whole line was about 30 miles (48 km) long, probably even more, and left us gasping at its potential. And all along it, blue oases in the green jungle, azure jewels in a shallow sea, lay Blue Holes.

Raleigh's Bahamian adventure staggered to an end. I returned to England and, for a while, had no interest in returning. Blue Holes had bled too much of my enthusiasm in the past few years, and I was feeling psychologically and financially battered by it all.

But it wasn't to be. Drawn increasingly by the environment itself – the wildlife, the geology, the mystery of the inner cave world, I wanted to see a decent accounting made of all the stories Blue Holes had to offer before I left them for others. Thus the Andros Project came about, an international scientific and exploration expedition which saw the largest team of expert divers and scientists yet brought together for a single research adventure to these underwater caves.

In 1986, we fielded a small reconnaissance team. Mary Stafford Smith and Sue Wells, two very experienced and very attractive marine biologists, came out to look at the life of the ocean holes, Peter Smart and Fiona Whittaker of Bristol University came to examine the geology and hydrology of the inland caves, and I came along as a sort of general dogsbody to do any actual cave diving that might be necessary. Over a one-month period, we found enough to convince us that a return with a larger team the following year was more than worth while. With each passing year, the Blue Holes were revealing more and more of their secrets, and a further picture of the caves and their enigmatic environment was beginning to emerge.

Some bits were disappointments. The actual entrances to the marine caves seemed to be little different to the patch reefs scattered throughout the shallows of the inner lagoon behind the barrier reef. But the life within the inner passages seemed more exciting, offering a different and cryptic environment to the biologists. Many of the species inside the caves were unusual, creatures less frequently found on the reefs outside, certainly at shallow, accessible depths.

The reversing currents remained somewhat of a mystery; there was no easy explanation for their existence, and it seemed that a complex interaction between rainwaters draining from the island, tidal differences on either side of the Banks (which create an actual 'head' of water alternately on opposite sides), and a sort of geothermal upwelling from beneath the Banks were between them responsible for the underground 'tides'. Winds and weather could also affect their change-over times. The difference in density between the colder, deeper water off the eastern coast and the shallower warmer water in the lagoons creates a sort of vertical circulation up through the edge of the island that means that caves have developed more readily on this eastern side of Andros.

The region at which the saline waters mixed with the fresh lens waters was still the greatest zone of cave development, and much of Pete Smart's work involved looking at the subtle changes that went on in the walls of the cave in this zone. The Blue Holes appeared to be an embryonic oilfield, the dissolution of the rock creating a great zone of porous limestone that, if surface conditions were ever right, might one day in the long distant future contain oil. Elsewhere in the world, there are ancient limestones that do now contain oil, and which seemed to have originally formed islands just like the Bahamas. We could actually swim inside the rocks – and the 'oilfields' – as they formed, and this excited scientists at Royal Dutch Shell enough to fund Pete's research.

Personally I found the biology of the inland caves was one of the most fascinating aspects. In the area just below the mixing zone, a host of tiny creatures exist in a well-defined hierarchy, most of which had a long ago adapted to a life of eternal darkness in the underworld. We had first come across these on Grand Bahama, where cave-diving biologists had confirmed the existence of many different species of previously unknown animals, some of which were effectively 'living fossils' now extinct in the outside world.

No one knew much about these at all, where they originally came from, how they bred and how they ate, whether they were unique to caves, or whether these too were an opportunistic population who had taken advantage of a particular supply of food, the organic wastes from the forests above that trickled down into the rock with the draining rainwaters. Some showed evidence of a deep-sea background, or had close family relatives down on the ocean bed.

They congregated beneath the sulphur layer like an underground rush-hour, where the smallest – ostracods, copepods and thermosbanaceans, tiny nektonic crustaceans – fed directly in the decaying, organic broth. Preying on these in turn, and adding omnivorously to their diet with the organic soup, larger crustaceans, isopods and amphipods and tiny shrimps, were the next rung up the ladder. At the top, the carnivores like *Remipedes* and free-swimming polychaete worms, munched most things in sight, though there was evidence that different species of *Remipedes*, apparently one of the oldest of the cave creatures, had adapted to feed on particular species of prey.

One of the few real discoveries made on Raleigh was that of a beautiful little 'polychaete', a delicate, free-swimming worm with long sensory appendages and little swimming paddles that made it look like a Viking longship, with oars and shield set in rows along its sides. A single 'horn' grew out of the centre of its head, and we nicknamed it 'Unicorn'. It had been found only once before, a few months earlier, in a cave in the nearby Turks and Caicos Islands. Its full Latin name is a real mouthful, *Pelago-macellicephala iliffi*. 'Unicorn' was a little easier.

South Andros Blue Holes were like underground zoos, there were more little troglobites than I had seen in almost any other Bahamian cave. Right at the top was our old friend *Lucifuga*, the blind cave fish, whose diet was no less opportunistic, being not averse to munching other *Lucifuga* when the opportunity arises.

Out in the forests on the north of the island, near Congo Town, we briefly explored one of the caves we had been unable to reach during Raleigh. The most southerly of the chain north of the airport, it was obviously used as a swimming hole by the local kids, as an old rope swing above the water testified. In the lake itself, the water was filled with tiny, delicate jellyfish, pulsing in the dusky waters in their apparent millions. How they got there, and remained, is a wonder. Perhaps trapped millennia ago by a falling sea, perhaps an individual carried in on the leg of a bird, but we had no real idea. They inhabit all the holes along the northerly group, but seem equally at home in the shallower brackish layers inside and outside of the dark caves. 'Jellyfish Lake' also contained some of the largest *Lucifuga* I'd ever seen, in caverns to north and south, old, battle-scarred individuals who lurked near the entrances, more pigmented than most.

Our interest in Blue Holes had come a long way from the simple beginnings of 'where does this cave go, and how far can I swim up it?' It had evolved into a branch of science and exploration all of its own, a unique combination of applied field research and pure exploration, and it had lost none of the thrill for all that. We still had the ephemeral pleasure, the utter fascination and delightful fear of exploring parts of the planet that no previous human had ever seen, in our adventurous pursuit of knowledge. There are few such opportunities left for man in the closing years of the twentieth century.

However, our main efforts during the Andros Project were to be centred on Stargate, the deep Blue Hole I had explored in 1985 to a depth of 200 ft (60 m), and along about 1,000 ft (300 m) of passages which ran both north and south of the entrance. Plumbed to 260 ft (78 m), we suspected it went much deeper.

The grandiose plan on the Andros Project was to hit it with everything we could muster. More than just to see where and how deep it went, we wanted to collect stalagmite samples from as deep as we could, and to collect wall rock and samples to see what effect the moving up and down of the mixing zone had on the structure of the limestone as it formed. Pretty esoteric stuff to most of us, but exploration is something that exists on many levels, not just in terms of humans 'being there'. Our scientific exploration was more valid in real terms than the simple 'let's see where it goes' type of adventure.

All this presented us with a major problem. To get to depths of over 200 ft (60 m) and work there safely and intelligently, we could not breathe compressed air, unless in a one-atmosphere suit, a pressurized, man-shaped submarine with arms. We thought about that for a while, but decided that such a suit would not allow the versatility and precision of movement we would need. Surface umbilicals, where breathing gas would be sent down a long hose from cylinders on the surface, posed a similar problem. They would be all right as part of a support system, but not as a primary breathing supply. The thought of dragging several hundred feet of weighty and unwieldy umbilical along the base of Stargate was appalling. Light-weight diving cylinders developed by Acurex for the Skylab programme, were a possibility, but time at depth is limited to how many cylinders one can carry. Although we had already used such lightweight open-circuit SCUBA very successfully in several locations, to depths of around 200 ft (60 m) in British caves, it had real limitations if the Bahamian caves went deeper. The idea was not simply to get a diver down a cave to 300 ft (90 m) plus, and bring him back, but to keep him there for a while and work him. We hoped to get even deeper – perhaps as far as 500 ft (150 m), if the Holes allowed. And still work.

Both Jochen Hasenmayer of Germany and Sheck Exley of the USA, probably the world's leading cave divers, have been down to 660 ft (200 m) in France's Fontaine de Vaucluse and Mexico's Nacimiento del Monte respectively, so we had no illusions about depth records. Using several diving tanks in stage systems, they had only seconds at that depth, a fleeting visit, touch and return. We intended to *work* at depths few cave divers had reached before. To do so, we went pretty much full circle, back to rebreathers, cousins of the simple breathing systems used in the earliest days of British cave diving.

Tomorrow's World is a British television programme that deals with interesting practical advances in applied technology. Sitting mulling over the deep-diving problem one evening, I was captivated by a short under-water sequence using mixed gas rebreathers, units which literally recycle the greater part of the gas mixture breathed by the diver. This allows a relatively small amount of breathing gas carried by the diver to last many times the limits imposed by 'open-circuit' systems, where the gas is exhaled into the surrounding water – simply 'thrown away' when used. The concept of rebreathers has been around since the 1940s, when simple oxygen units were used with great success during the war on sabotage missions. Early units were relatively unreliable, and the problems associated with later developments in rebreather technology have kept prices high and avail-ability limited.

Those on *Tomorrow's World* looked exactly what we needed. They were basically systems designed by an American company, Rexnord, and these had been mentioned by several experts in diving technology I had approached as possible equipment to use. But as far as anyone knew, all the Rexnord rebreathers in existence were owned by the US or Israeli Navies, and they were military units which we had no chance of obtaining.

The television programme mentioned Fort Bovisand at Plymouth, and the Diving Diseases Research Centre, run by Dr Maurice Cross, a rather notorious figure who worked on the applied side of decompression-related research. I had met Maurice before, during deep-diving exercises in Wookey Hole and Gavel Pot, two of Britain's deepest underwater caves. Maurice seemed to regard us in the same manic light that the bulk of the diving world regarded him, but so far our 100 per cent safety record on open-circuit mixed-gas cave-diving reassured him that we stood just on the acceptable side of the sanity line. A couple of days later, I rang him to ask who owned the rebreathers. Maurice wasn't there, but his assistant, Jane Pimlock, answered the phone. The conversation proved to be a little more direct than I was expecting.

'Hi there, Jane, who owns the rebreathers that were on *Tomorrow's World* last week?'

'Hi, Rob, a company called Carmellan Research. Their Managing Director is standing next to me right now. I'll put him on.'

There's a certain difficulty in making an instant approach for support without actually thinking about what you are going to say beforehand! I found myself talking with Stuart Clough of Carmellan, who fortunately had seen our Conch Sound television programme and knew something of our work. As luck would have it, they were looking for somewhere more challenging to undertake field trials with the units, and after a meeting a few days later, Stuart offered Carmellan's help with the Project, if we would cover their basic expenses.

There was all the difference in the world between the early ex-MOD air rebreathers, used in the 1940s in early cave-dives at Wookey Hole and elsewhere, and the modern Carmellan-Rexnord ones we arranged to use on Andros. Our ones were designed to work at depths of up to 1,500 ft (450 m), for several hours at a stretch. They used sensors and simple computing software within the unit to calculate the amount of oxygen and 'diluent' (the other gas in the breathing mixture: in air, this is nitrogen; in our mixture it was helium) needed to keep a set amount of oxygen in the breathing mixture at whatever depth the diver happened to be at the time. The Carmellan breathing mixtures used a slightly greater concentration of oxygen than in the air we breathe at the surface, and this was suitable only if bottom times were comparatively short. This mixture would be toxic if breathed for long durations at such depths – oxygen is actually poisonous if breathed for long at pressures greater than surface pressure (1 atmosphere) – but was fine for brief, deep excursions. It also had the benefit of reducing our decompression times significantly. Decompression tables specifically for his mix had been worked out in advance by Carmellan's cohort in the States, Dr Bill Hamilton of Hamilton Research, and tested exhaustively in 'dry-dives' by Maurice and the Carmellan divers inside recompression chambers at the Diving Diseases Research Centre at Fort Bovisand. Rob Parker and I joined Stuart and Neil Cave, his chief diver, for a training programme that involved a series of 'dry-dives' in the Bovisand recompression chamber to depths of 500 ft (150 m), breathing heliox from the rebreathers.

In 1987, rebreathers were used to explore deeper caves. Rob Palmer and Rob Parker undertake a 'dry' training dive to 500 ft (150 m) with Neil Clough of Carmellan Research, at the Diving Diseases Research Centre at Fort Bovisand. *(Photo: Gavin Newman)*

Stargate was a far cry from standard diving sites. Its remoteness meant that, effectively, we were on our own if something went wrong, and our planning had to take this into account. To cope with the unlikely but possible chance of system failure, the rebreather divers would each carry an extra high-pressure cylinder of heliox, enough to run away on if a serious problem arose with one of the sets (although the rebreathers themselves had several failsafe backup systems built in). An umbilical hose, with two Apeks valves on the end, would be hung down to 70 ft (21 m) so that escaping divers could switch to a mixture system that could be controlled from the surface, allowing oxygen levels to increase as the depth decreased. These would also be used from 30 ft (9 m) upwards on each dive, to supply pure oxygen to the divers during the final stages of decompression. An inflatable one-man recompression chamber was lent by SOS Ltd in case of decompression sickness, though, if possible, we intended to evacuate an oxygen-breathing drip-fed casualty by helicopter to the AUTEC chamber on North Andros, about 40 miles (64 km) away. We had arranged emergency helicopter cover with AUTEC through the Royal Navy, and a further Medivac facility for a really serious incident, where a badly bent or injured diver could be taken to the US Naval chambers in Panama City, in North Florida, some 500 miles (800 km) away.

Finally, a small Phantom 500 ROV (remote operated vehicle) was borrowed from Deep Ocean Engineering in California, with the idea of enabling us to see what surprises might lie in store before divers were committed to the water. All this equipment was available for a limited time, and had to be airfreighted in. British Airways and Eastern Airlines very generously sponsored the flights. It was to be by no means an easy logistical operation.

The entrance to Stargate, with the awning slung up to protect the divers and their support team from the unpleasant midday heat. *(Photo: Chris Howes FRPS)*

Richard Stevenson, with air cylinders slung on his sides in British cave diving fashion, floats in front of a cascade of underwater crystal formations, over 100 ft (30m) down in Stargate. *(Photo: Rob Palmer)*

Rob Parker in the water at Stargate, on the rebreather dive that took him and Stuart Clough to a depth of 320 ft (96m) in the cave. *(Photo: Chris Howes FRPS)*

Stargate – the enormous North Passage, at a depth of 120 ft (36m). Below the divers, the cave walls plummet to a depth of over 250 ft (75m), to reach a floor of huge jumbled boulders. Beneath these, the cave continues to unknown depths. *(Photo: Bill Stone)*

An Arawak Indian skull, 70 ft (20m) underwater in Sanctuary Blue Hole. The distinctive flattened forehead indicates its origin. *(Photo: Rob Palmer)*

Bernard Picton floats in Mohebi Hall in Sanctuary, in front of a tall, strangely-shaped stalagmite on the central 'island'. *(Photo: Rob Palmer)*

Grazing along the cave wall in Porcupine Hole, a measle cowrie makes a meal of the tiny organisms anchored to the wall itself. *(Photo: Chris Howes FRPS)*

Silhouetted by the branching fingers of gorgonians, a diver sinks into the depths of one of the spectacular Blue Holes of Andros. *(Photo: Rob Palmer)*

Rob Palmer with the skeletal remains of a turtle found several hundred feet into Rat Cay Blue Hole. *(Photo: Martyn Farr)*

CHAPTER EIGHT

The Andros Project: Avalon and Stargate

COMING BACK to Andros again in 1987 was a mixed experience. Six years on from the first expedition to Conch Sound, I'd begun to learn my lesson, and had delegated much of the work to others. Ian Bishop, our Project Manager, was with me when we got to Deep Creek on South Andros, ready to get to grips with island life after several hectic days of bureaucracy in Nassau. Things got off to a fine start as we steamed into the harbour at Deep Creek on the MV *Delmar*, the local inter-island cargo boat, which promptly ground to a premature halt with several feet of mooring cable around its propellor. My first hour on Andros was spent with a 100 cu. ft (8.5 cu. m) diving tank wedged between my knees as I slowly sawed the rope away with the cook's carving knife. The locals on the concrete pier and the *Delmar*'s crew chatted casually to each other from the shade of palms and boat deck as if this were a pretty normal occurrence, which it probably was.

Trying to run a large expedition composed of a mixed bag of scientists, divers, general field workers and hangers-on leaves little time for appreciating these finer delights of island life. Several years of familiarity with Andros life meant that I had forgotten the sheer novelty of the place. Not so Chris Howes. Chris, our official photographer, was an old friend from Welsh caving days, who had blossomed over the years into one of the finest adventure and natural history photographers I knew. He arrived mid-expedition and his eye for detail brought my own earliest memories to life again.

Chris Howes: My first impressions of the island didn't even begin with Andros itself. Judith Calford and I flew out to Miami, then onwards at dusk to Nassau. Nassau, in comparison to Miami, was a less salubrious airport, cooling tarmac outside and a hot-house within. Facilities were basic, we were tired. A few paltry conveyers belts ran, for the most part carrying cardboard boxes of Pampers, a couple of Michelin tyres, electric fans, a broken picture. Miami is cheaper to shop in than Nassau, even including the air fare.

There followed a leisurely drive across town, past the shanty buildings and Bay Street, where the cruise ships dock and the tourists flock by day. The town has a one-way system; you see the tourist trap with the T-shirt shops on the way in, the back streets and the shanties on return.

We finally reached the quay – not the huge ocean-liner port, but the real centre of activity. This is where the first genuine impressions of a different culture made themselves felt. We were to catch the mail boat, a nondescript tub that lay against the wharf. A single gangplank rose from the concrete, narrow and unstable, to allow entry to the almost-as-narrow portal 6 ft (1.8 m) above. Our guide, a local diver who had met us at the airport, aimed us in the right direction and left us to it.

We had heavy dive bags and little knowledge of what was expected. The first thing, getting on the boat, was more difficult than it might sound. Heaving up the bags was hard, becoming harder when they totally blocked the passage that led inwards, the aisle down the centre of the boat. Native Bahamians struggled past us in frustration, hot in the humid confines. Everywhere there were people. The Captain came along, flicking his fingers.

'We full up, no room.'

I stared. There was only the one boat a week to Andros. He started back across the mound of luggage we had manhandled aboard. He waved vaguely towards the entrance, out of sight round the corner.

'No room left, all tickets sold.' I had visions for a moment that we would be left stranded in the docks, watching our connection with our friends depart. Inspiration was required.

'Would you check, there should be something booked. We're diving, working for the Government.' It must have sounded ludicrous enough. He got his book from his mate, who looked through it idly, then repeated that there was no room, and wandered away. We took our chance, not really believing that there was no room for passengers – perhaps he thought we wanted one of the squalid cabins. Dragging the bags, we got them to the end of the corridor, out of the way on the seaward side.

A narrow door on to the walkway around the ship was blocked, as was the whole walkway, with rows of propane cylinders. The boat was ringed with them, freight for the Family Islands. Send in your orders, collect from the shore. It looked uncomfortable, but offered the only way to hide and get out of the way. I crawled out over the jutting tops of bottles, dropping cameras down between them into the grease and oil which covered my jeans for the rest of the month. Bags finally resided on top, and I could sit, bowed beneath the low ceiling made by the upper deck. The air was still, carrying noises of the quayside activity. Beyond, there was an arching bridge carrying traffic to Paradise Island, the occasional boat conveying dancing tourists back to shore. There was money over the water!

To have slept the night there would have been purgatory. Judith looked after the bags, I climbed out over the side of the ship to clutch at the pitted railings above and haul myself upwards, rolling on to the upper deck in front of the bridge. Was I meant to be here? No one challenged me, so I walked back past the cabins to the stern.

The *Captain Moxey* leaves Kemps Bay for its nine hour journey to Nassau. *(Photo: Rob Palmer)*

Here, cargo was strewn about. A car blocked the rear gangway down, if there ever was one. The locals seemed to know their way about, throwing up bicycles over the rails to be caught by their fellows. An acrid smoke belched out of a hatch, oil fumes swirling round the tarpaulins. Yes, we could sleep better here than on the bottles.

Judith pushed the bags up, and I hauled them across to a point below the bridge windows. It was calmer here, with no fumes. If we got moved, so be it. We hadn't learnt the laid-back ways of the Bahamian yet – no-one cared about such things. Their friendliness was outstanding. But we'd had no chance to acclimatize to the different society. Exhausted, we lay down on the bags, arms through straps, and wondered what the next stage of the long journey would bring.

On the quay, more people had gathered. Throughout the hour, the ship's loudspeakers had blared reggae over the docks. There was a steady thump of music which reverberated through the boat. I could see one man open a car boot, lifting out a small cardboard box of something, by the dim light spilling from the cabins and the headlamps of the cars parked nearby. The cars were scattered, no ranks or order to them, another instance of the Bahamian attitude. More power to them. As the musical beat took hold, he took one dancing pace backwards, three forward, two back. Progress was slow, but obviously enjoyed. Shipping items to Andros was more than a mere delivery.

We never did discover any steps to the upper deck, and few Bahamians came up, climbing as we did over the side. Those that did slept, like us, on the floor – better than the fetid conditions below, where people paid extra for the privilege of a crowded bunkroom. The wind and spray, which were picking up, were far more pleasant. We even had a visit from an expatriate Brit, Joy Chaplin, with messages and gifts to be conveyed to the expedition. Then, promptly at 11.00 pm, the quay was left behind, the reggae silenced, and once away from the lights the stars appeared by their millions until the gathering clouds occluded them.

By dawn we were both uncomfortable, tired after only a couple of hours' sleep, and famished. A squashed Mars bar, deported from Britain, did little to banish the hunger pangs. The sun came up like a children's drawing, rays of light streaming in an arc towards the lightening sky. Neither of us had ever seen anything like it before. One rotund Bahamian wandered up to see us photographing it. He was short, barrel-like, and hardly spoke. I didn't know how to take him. He grinned and gestured, patted his belly and giggled. Was he implying that I had a pot?

By now, Andros was coming into sight. As we neared, people started to wake and come out from below, handing off the railings of the lower deck. Rows of them sat on the crates marked 'This Way Up', though you would have had to stand on your head to read it. 'Do Not Crush', read others, bucking under their weight. Cardboard, the universal Bahamian protection, strikes again. Fridges seemed to be the 'in' thing for this voyage – we found out later that South Andros had just entered the twentieth century with the building of a power plant. Power to the people indeed! Electrical goods to follow.

The channel into the small harbour was marked with poles and pylons, encrusted with life. Sea grass was clearly visible on the sand; a turtle swam away, frenetic activity in the calm sea. The dots on land resolved themselves into people, just as the heat began to build up. One white body stood out among the locals – Ian Bishop was there to meet us, catching our bags as we hurled them down. He was already tanned, wearing shorts, and covered with mosquito bites. I quickly learned that most of the indigenous insect population was either eating you, trying to eat you, thinking of eating you, was already full up, or squashed. The former categories greatly outnumbered the latter.

By the time we got to the 'base camp', a small group of three concrete buildings by the sea, the Andros day was in full swing, hot and humid. The accommodation was overcrowded. Of the three rooms in the main building, one was an overflowing bunkroom, another the toilet (flushable, if you got the bucket of seawater filled first), and the last one the communal everything else. Cooking, battery charging, eating, film processing, sleeping, all went on here. We were shown our sleeping quarters, the porch, and the darkroom-to-be, otherwise known as the loo. I somehow didn't think it would be a good idea to seal myself for hours at a time into the only relief the expedition had! I might not become too popular, interred like that.

Rob Palmer: Chris arrived when things were at their busiest. By common consensus we found him another darkroom, across in the 'Laboratory'. No one really wanted to queue up to defecate. We were, in fact, lucky to have a base at all. Our original hope had been to obtain use of the secondary-school buildings at Deep Creek, but despite the qualified agreement of the local headmaster, we could raise no enthusiasm from the Ministry in Nassau. Our good friends on the island, Stan and Dorothy Clarke, had found another possibility, but when Stan, Ian and I called in on our arrival, this too had fallen through. There was one recourse, the old buildings Stan had built to live in when he first retreated to Andros, but which had been recently sold to an off-island owner. These hadn't really been lived in for about ten years, but a couple of phone calls from Stan soon had us taking down shutters and sweeping skeletal centipedes from the bath, and other such dusty corners.

The Andros Project base camp at Deep Creek, beside the only road on South Andros. *(Photo: Chris Howes FRPS)*

It was something of a far cry from the space and relative comfort we had hoped for from the school buildings, but it was by the road and by the sea, ideal for boats and vehicles. We had Honda generators to provide power, and Ian strung cables and hooked up gas cylinders while I used our power strimmer to clear bush and shrubbery from the out-buildings. What freight we had with us, brought in on the local cargo boat, we either stored near the pier or brought down, trying to get the place a little lived in before the rest of the team started arriving.

I rather liked the place; three blue concrete blockhouses, ventilated by open, screen windows (fine if the wind blew, not so fine if it didn't) each with a porch that faced the sea and the dawn. The main building lay right by the road; another, which we made our laboratory and darkroom, lay a little behind and to one side. Dark pink and blue flowers were scattered in the patchwork of grass and rock that surrounded the hut, and the jungle started a little behind the back door, beyond the brackish well. The third building, our dive store, and home for Bill and Pat Stone, lay across the road, a little above the beach. Offshore, an old cylinder block was buoyed to give anchorage for our Zodiacs, and by the time a couple of days had been spent on the site, it began to look almost homely. Hammocks were strung between coconut palms on the beach, a barbecue was erected, we had gas cookers and both 120 v and 240 v electricity, a compressor shack and showers (albeit brackish and somewhat dependent on water availability).

Compared with many expeditions I had been on, these surroundings bordered on the luxurious. It is actually pretty easy to tell who has been on expedition seriously before. Those who have simply wince and keep quiet. Those who haven't, winge. Unfortunately, we had to cram up to two dozen people on site at one point during the first month, which was about a dozen more than comfortable. Surprisingly few people winged.

Ian and I worked flat out for the first two days, making it liveable in. 'Bish's' enthusiasm was buoyed up by continual promises of forthcoming dives in the sea, always 'in a couple of hours, when we've finished this job . . .'. By the end of the second day, a curious resignation had crept into his features. Expedition christening, I guess. His sense of humour was restored considerably on day three.

Morning on Andros generally hit us as the sun rose. A mixture of heat, insects, and the generator running out of fuel usually got us up at dawn. On day three I stumbled through the back door, barefoot and naked, rubbing the sleep from my eyes, and wandered into the forest to ablute. Hidden from the road by thick undergrowth, I yawned mightily and peed copiously over a shrub, blinking at a big black and yellow spider on a dew-spattered web in front of my nose. It slowly dawned on me that the shrub was objecting to my actions. The branches writhed, and jerked away. Focusing blearily on it, I froze in mid-spray. A small brown snake stared balefully back at me, dripping with urine, and winding itself for the spring.

The sight and sound of me screaming, and leaping backwards through the bushes stark naked, member still in hand and closely followed by an outraged small brown snake, sent Bish quite hysterical. Safe in the house, my backside still smarting from the thorny scrub, I pointed out with a sort of nervous justification that, though the snake, a 'Brown Racer', was not actually lethal it had been known to hurt people. While, as a back-fanged viper, a finger would have to be stuck pretty far down its throat for it to get its teeth into and inject venom, there was one part of the human anatomy that sort of resembled a finger in general proportion, and that was the bit that had effectively 'attacked' the snake, as far as it was concerned. Bish merely remarked, the tears in his eyes obviously echoing his concern, that I would at least have had an interesting scar to show at parties.

The team arrived in dribs and drabs. First came Bill and Pat Stone, from Washington, and Richard Stevenson, Ian Kelly, Fiona Whittaker and Rob Parker from England. Rob was a veteran of Blue Holes expeditions, with three previous visits under his belt. He and I had been to South Andros together in 1982, on our way to Conch Sound, and he had left a few loose ends he wanted to get back to. Richard was a cave-diver from Wookey, in Somerset, and he and I had been working together on a project beneath the limestone cliffs of Cheddar Gorge, the exploration of the legendary 'Lost Cave of Cheddar'. Richard was in charge of our electrics, and had worked hard with Mike Spellar of Aquabeam to produce special lighting systems, Andros Lights, for the Project. Ian, 'Yanto' to his friends, was the extrovert brother of Bish's girlfriend, and our base camp manager. A rabid skydiver, his parachute was on his shoulder as he leapt ashore, intent on finding a local pilot to drop him over the island. Fiona was a hydrologist, studying the water chemistry of the caves, and had been out the year before on the reconnaissance trip. Bill and Pat were cave divers from the States, who had worked on explorations with Rob Parker in Wookey Hole in England, and on deep-cave dives in Mexico. Bill was one of the USA's best deep-cave divers and technicians, and one of the foremost authorities on mixed-gas diving underground. Quite a bunch. Ian and I greeted them on the dock with cold beers at 7.00 pm, allowed them to throw us in the water, and took them home.

Already, familiar problems were beginning to appear. The oxygen and helium suppliers, so vital to our deep-diving programme, were still in Miami. A long and protracted sponsorship arrangement with Air Products had ensured their availability, but a change of management in the Miami office had ground things to a halt. The new manager had come in on his first day, looked at the arrangement, postponed it, and promptly made himself uncontactable by going off househunting. By the time we had worked round him, with phone-calls flying between Andros, England and North America, it was obvious that we were going to be several days behind schedule. It didn't help that Bill had left the vital Haskel Booster Pump back in Washington, the device that would jack up air pressures from the Air Products storage cylinders to those required by our own diving tanks and the Carmellan rebreathers. I had arranged to pick this up in Miami on my way through, but a confusion over delivery meant that it arrived back in Washington at Bill's house a week after I had left. Bill, not hearing from me, assumed that I had made other arrangements, and, with an already enormous mound of equipment to bring, left it behind. On Andros I simply assumed that, as it had obviously gone to Washington, Bill would automatically bring it down. We sat unhappily over a beer, each feeling the other was more to blame, and wondered how to get it here.

Bill tried phoning friends to arrange air-freight and to buy and send vital spare parts to marry it to our air compressors, and we entered one of those appalling limbos where, promises having been made, we had to sit tight and wait and see. So we started diving with our ordinary SCUBA tanks. Bill and Rob went with Fiona to see Stargate and take water samples before it was disturbed by regular diving, while Richard and I went off to dive the lake at the northern end of a large area of collapse containing two Blue Holes behind High Rock Primary School.

'Oh damn it. I've forgotten my bloody fins,' Richard gasped incredulously. Sweat fell in streamlets from his brows. He staggered backwards on to the small sloping ledge by the water's edge, and sat down with a definitive clank.

'Shit,' he said, disbelievingly.

For the past hour, we'd been struggling back and forth through the bush from the road, carrying our diving equipment across an appalling area of broken limestone slopes where every step held the opportunity for a slip into a pothole or crevice. Here, sharp 'love-vines' draped invisibly between thorn bushes tore the hell out of traipsing ankles, and poisonwood lurked between slightly more innocuous (if utterly thick and impenetrable) scrub to provide trick handholds for desperately grasping fingers. The late-afternoon sun warmed the wings of mosquitoes and doctor-flies, as they sucked high tea from our bare shoulders. Somehow, the two of us managed to lower the gear down a cleft to the water's edge, and kitted up on a small, sloping platform, finishing the job in the warm, soupy water itself. This was the first 'exploration' dive of 1987. Small annoying problems with equipment kept us in a state of stimulated annoyance. Habits had not yet adjusted to expedition-mode, and this was the time when things go wrong.

For Richard, the tribulations of the day went unrewarded. Locked sweatily inside hundreds of pounds worth of specialized diving gear, he finally observed that his fins were still back at base.

Bad luck, Richard, I thought, floating beneath the overhanging wall at the far side of the Blue Hole. By now, my own little troublesome moments had left me wanting only to get underwater, explore, and go home. Richard glared across the pool.

'Go and have a dive,' he said through clenched teeth. I nodded in mute understanding. Now was not a good time to be around Richard.

'See you in a bit, then,' I said, and quickly swam off alone to see where, if anywhere, the lake went.

This was the northern end of the 'School Hole' collapse. The polluted waters of School Hole itself lay across a separating barrier of thick rushes, giant, prehistoric ferns and algae-covered boulders, a tangle of mangroves and salt-resistant shrubs. Jungle, in short. Pigeons and grey herons and great orange butterflies flew between the trees, nesting in the greenery. On the walls of a cave at the far northern end of the lake, crabs and lizards and great grey-and-yellow spiders scuttered amongst gnarled brown mudstones which curled in dull corroded fingers from the lichenous roof. I stuck my head underwater. The tannic liquid drank in my lights like a sponge. Oh, God, eucch!

I followed the west wall down, past whorls of bacteria that filled the water like pallid galaxies in a great brown universe. Lumps of fetid algae drifted down from above, infallibly and inevitably retracing the route of my ascending air bubbles. The wall ended on a steep debris slope, where leaves, algae and branches blended in soft, enthusiastic decay. The rotten-egg smell of hydrogen sulphide permeated my mouthpiece. Isn't death wonderful? I followed the slope down for quite a way, to bare rocks and clear water, 70 ft (20 m) below the surface. There I took breath, floating carefully in the water, very aware that sudden careless movements would completely ruin my visibility, losing any chance I had of finding the way on.

At first the boulder blockage seemed complete. Two tiny cave dwellers, thermosbanaceans, swam in the water between the rocks, a tantalizing hint of clear cave beyond. There was only one constricted gap that could possibly offer a way through, and it looked loose. Blocks hung poised above it in delicate suspension. Perhaps sideways, head first, I could carefully jackknife through. The things we do in desperation. With one hand outstretched, grasping reel, my camera and lamphead, I wriggled cautiously through, paint scraping from my tanks as I did so. 'Mung', the decaying algal-bacterial gunge that fills these waters in an organic blizzard of brown snow, swept in behind me, instantly obscuring any view of the way out. I turned carefully round, moving by touch in the blind mists of the confined boulder pile, and tried to ensure that the line ran through the tiny opening, and not through cracks on one side. Unless the visibility settled before I tried to get out, then passing the constriction might prove my undoing. There was no belay for the line, and I simply had to place it in the opening, and hope it would stay. Touch is an interesting sense, but ideally it's designed to be used in conjunction with sight.

I turned again, to the cave. The passage was small, only a yard or so in diameter, and undulated in sandy limestone over a silty floor. The walls were clean, and the floor rose to a small chamber, where the silt turned to sand, and I could pause to take stock of the situation. I checked my air supplies, and both regulators, to make sure everything was working after the silt and the squeeze. Fine. I looked round. The passage had an air of freshness about it as though more recently formed than the deeper, larger caves. But a small corroded run of flowstone trickled down one wall, so the newness was an illusion. I was almost 100 ft (30 m) down, if this cave was here when such flowstone could form, it must be at least 20,000 years old. Older than me. I tied the line to a rock on the floor, and put the camera down, feeling there was little I could photograph here. I swam over the chamber, into a rift, and looked down. The bright sandy floor disappeared. I felt a twinge of vertigo. The floor simply didn't exist. There was just a void, the walls disappearing into the depths, an almost physical suction dragging me over the edge.

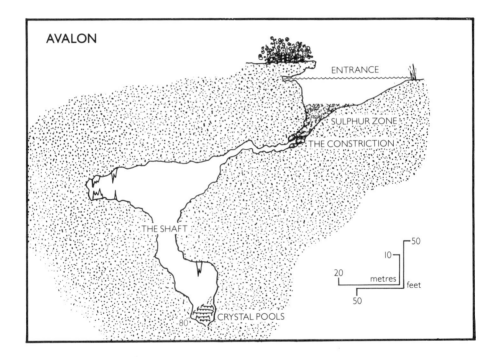

I hung back and checked my gauges again, through fear if nothing else. Rushing into things isn't a good habit. I looked long and hard at the walls, the roof and my depth gauge, settling myself. Then, with a deep breath, I slowly dived forward, bleeding air from my suit to descend. Great draperies of stalactite flowed by me down the walls, tiny white animals swam past in the crystal water, and the cave was still going on down. Directly ahead, the walls pinched in, and a ledge at -130 ft (-40 m) gave me a reference point. I tied the line reel to a small stalagmite, and paused for breath. Time to change mouthpieces, one tank was already a third down. Beneath my fins, dark water beckoned. The temptation was too great. Reasoning that I still needed time to allow the entrance to clear, I exhaled and threw my arms and legs out, sky-diving, space-walking, drifting down through a gap at 170 ft (50 m) to emerge in the roof of a chamber, 60 ft (18 m) long and 20 ft (6 m)

wide. My eyes flicked back and forth from cave to depth gauge, trying to take in the view and maintain an awareness of where I actually was. The needle on the gauge crept to 250 ft (75 m). I stopped, hanging weightless in mid-water, the floor below only 10–15 ft (3–4.5 m) below me.

And what a floor! Cascading down the eastern wall, a pure white river of flowstone broke out into crystal gour pools, terraces of frozen calcite that crept across the floor in descending pools of glory towards a tiny opening at the base of the western wall. Aeons ago, when the oceans dropped to greater depths than this, a stream of rainwater must have carried dissolved limestone down the wall into the dry chamber. Some of this evaporated out in the drier atmosphere of the cave, forming calcite waterfalls and the cascading, crystal pools below. Great sharp-edged fingers of pure calcite lay in the 'gours', where water once pooled behind a calcite dam. The final trickle that crept over the last barrier ran into the hole in the floor, a tiny opening that seemed too small for man.

A large white isopod swam by, less than 0.5 in (1.27 cm) long, tiny 'legs' and tail flickering in rapid motion. A few solitary thermosbanaceans, tiny sediment feeders more usually found at shallower depths, hung in the transparent waters. I wondered whether the deep cave was a resting place from the busier waters above. But not for me. I was far beyond where I should be, utterly out of my environment, with no spare decompression tank above, and my second tank was now also on its 'third' mark. I blew air into my suit, and began the long rise up through the gap, to follow the thin guideline towards the constriction and the outside world.

The squeeze was a bitch. Cords and hoses got stuck, more paint rasped from the tanks, but I got through. My decompression stops were all in the sulphur layer, and the rotten-egg taste crept continuously past the regulator into my mouth. I hung there for an hour, creeping slowly up the wall, to wedge myself under a ledge at −10 ft (−3 m) and lapse into a near doze. I broke surface almost at sunset, to find Richard in the water, hiding from the bugs. My skin was wrinkled from the long dive; red sulphur deposits coated the hairs on my hands. It felt good to breathe clean air again.

Why do we give caves names? I guess that by personifying things, we make them more real to us. We give them boundaries. We pretend understanding. Also, we get a buzz out of being clever. Some people make it simple. North Passage, East Chamber, Lower Level. Even Mount Everest, Bering Straits, Williamsburg. No imagination at all. Here I am. I found this. I'll name it after me. How did we ever get down from the trees?

I'm an unashamed romantic. If somewhere really stuns me with its glory, it deserves a decent name: Stargate, Elvenhome; back in Britain, in places that meant a lot to me, there was Radagast's Revenge and Puddleglum's Paradise, each an utterly different place; Ardfinnan's Reward (think about it) in Eire, Lothlorien and Helm's Deep on Grand Bahama – all parts of the planet that fascinate me, which I feel deserve better than disinterested definition. These are places that man did not build, they're not just north of here, south of there, above or under that. They existed thousands of years before our ancestors worked out how to smack stones together and kill people. To name something millennia-old and beautiful without due recourse to imagination seems somehow ridiculous. But each to their own. If men or women did something special, or really out of the ordinary . . . well, names are sort of transitory after all, generations change and forget. But at least be inventive, make the names mean something.

So perhaps I should have named this something Bahamian. But what? The Bahamas have little in the way of legend. There was potential elsewhere for Chickcharnie Cave, Mermaid's Lair. Mythology is universal, every civilization has lost lands, forgotten dreams. Through mists, and through rocks, to reach a dark well and a crystal lake. It reminded me of home, in England, where I lived within 20 miles from Glastonbury, the ancient source of legend, as did Richard. This submerged, lost land, with its deep crystal lakes, became the Bahamian Avalon.

But not everything comes so easily. The bare details of expedition work are more abrupt. The early days of the Andros Project offered little in the way of relaxation, and I spent most of my time above water, rather than within it.

How did we manage to exist and work under such confined, intense conditions? Expedition work would be a tremendous psychological study, presuming that good psychologists could themselves cope with the conditions. Few can, most prefer to pontificate from homely rooms in civilized climes. Cave-diving expeditions must be more rewarding than most, cave divers being a somewhat intense breed, and the Andros Project was many things to many people. Some were there to explore to go into new places, to revel in the physical excitement of sheer discovery. Others were there for similar reasons, though their exploration was less physical, taken in brief forays of scientific delight. Some were there to work, to undertake a certain, defined programme of toil, in which the environment was simply another part of the planet to be in. Some were there for fun, for the fascination of being somewhere new. Almost all were doing something different. And each needed to be understood.

I have my own reasons for being there. But because they are a mixture of most of the above, I can appreciate why others do it, though this took awhile, several years of misunderstanding and getting it wrong, of muddling through, and occasionally losing people I had thought were friends in the process. But now, though it must seem that I dabble in disciplines, I gain a better understanding about why the caves are there, and what they are, each time I dive. I still spend much of my time on each expedition hoping that people will work together more than they do, that they will somehow empathically understand why I ask them there, that they will accept the conditions they work in because the rewards, for the initiated, are immense. I can think of few other places on Earth where, this late in mankind's exploration of his planet, there are still unseen places to go, new discoveries to make.

But we all are human. There are more mundane reasons, which are probably just as valid. Stuart and the Carmellan team were there to work on the field performance of their equipment and were learning lessons they didn't expect to. Bill was there to discover more about deep diving, and rebreathers in particular. Rob was there because he wanted to be, and he wanted to be the best he possibly could. Between us, we formed the core of the Project, whether we liked it or not.

So ask anyone on the team why we were there, and a different answer would come with each query. The central concept was to find out as much as we could about Blue Holes – they are, after all, some of the world's most exciting natural phenomena. Of those who had the authority to call the tunes, Pete Smart and Sarah Cunliffe were jingling their purses, and looking hard at the piper. Which was me.

Pete had a lot depending on his work. Not only was Shell Exploration, one of the biggest geological research organizations funding the research, but the British National Environment Research Council (NERC) were putting a great deal of funding into the deep diving side of the project. Pete needed to recover stalagmites from depth, and the cash for the rebreather project had come from his efforts.

Sarah, however, had her own career resting on the successful outcome of the film. Though she had, in a previous 'incarnation', been the biologist on one of our Grand Bahama Blue Hole expeditions, she now worked for Oxford Scientific Films, and was directing the filming of the Andros Project for National Geographic Television. Though less hard cash had come in from the National Geographic film, much goodwill from sponsors rested on it.

Any major expedition like ours has several public facets. Personally, I feel that unless humanity gets the best go at learning as much as it can from my work, then I'm failing. That means that not only must science get what it can, in hard facts, but the great mass of the 'general public' must also get something too. Hence the film. Unless people think it's special, all the scientific papers in the world mean nothing. And unless science agrees its interest, public opinion matters not. Such, like it or not, is the balance of real, applied discovery.

Anyway, here I was, playing 'piggy-in-the-middle', with scientists, film crew and divers all wondering when things were really going to start happening, and all crying their importance. No sign of breathing gases, no Haskel Booster Pump, no deep diving. Andros is a long way from anywhere, when it really comes to it. Phone calls from the island, though an interesting social experience, leave the caller frustrated. Nothing was happening. I flew to Nassau.

Sitting on the end of a decent phone in the National Trust offices, with no one to offer alternative plans around me, was a delight. A day's hard bargaining and a short meeting with 'Tippy' Lightbourne of Cavalier Shipping, saw the gases on the boat from Florida to Nassau under sponsorship, with a promise of immediate delivery to the Andros cargo boat. Returning to Andros, I was faced with a succession of days in which problems simply mounted – our transport broke down, we had to hire extra vehicles, the gas arrived but the Haskel didn't, people unused to such basic field conditions took time adjusting, to the irritation of others. The Haskel was the most serious problem, people's social demands took second place. There it was, sitting in Bill's cellar in Washington, shiny and bright and new, boxed-up and all ready to use. There we were, sitting in Andros, a thousand miles away. None of Bill's contacts seemed to be able to get it on a plane and down here. We sat unhappily over another beer, and thought about it again.

The 1987 Andros Project team. Sea to shore:

John Hutchison, Yanto, Brad Pecel, Keith Turner, Rob Parker, Rob Palmer, Paul Hutchison, Chris Howes (kneeling), John Mylroie, Isobel Fairclough, Dave Whiteside, Fiona Whittaker, Ian Bishop (sitting), Jim Carew, Pat Stone, Bill Stone, Pete Smart, Judith Calford, Stuart Clough, Neil Cave, Sharon Yskamp, Richard Stevenson, Grace Niska, Paul Atkins and Sarah Cunliffe. (Not shown: Rob Trott, Bernard Picton, Bill Hamilton, Peter Glanvill) *(Photo: Chris Howes FRPS)*

Near Bill, next state down, lived a cave diver called Roberta Swicegood, whom we both knew well. One of us, I can't remember which, suggested we ring her and ask her to fly down with it. We grinned rather despairingly at each other. Roberta was a go-for-it person. She'd do it. Only trouble is, before she came, she would ring round the whole US cave-diving establishment and have a good laugh at our predicament.

Which she did, but she also arrived on Andros with the Booster within twenty-four hours of our call. We were stunned at her efficiency, and overjoyed. Bill got to work immediately, connected things wrongly and blew himself up, got to work again, fixed it, and we were moving.

As soon as we were operational, Stuart and Neil decanted enough gas into the rebreathers to make a foray into Mars Bay Blue Hole, a deep *cenote* that lay right on the beach at the end of the road on South Andros. Rob and I had dived down inside the huge bell-shaped dome to −200 ft (−60 m) in 1982, touching the tip of a sand cone at 180 ft (54 m), beyond which the cave sloped on down into unknown depths. Before the rebreather dive, Rob and Bill dropped down with a shortline, to find the cone tip at −170 ft (−50 m). The cave seemed to be filling in. On a second dive they went on to reach a point further down the slope to −240 ft (−72 m), and there it seemed as though the cave were beginning to level out. Suddenly it became more than just a game. This was now a potentially deep site that might give us the rewards we were after. They decanted pure oxygen into spare tanks for decompressing on at their shallower stops, and went back to the beach, with air tanks pumped higher than they should be for extra duration.

Bill's diary: Rob [Parker] and I loaded the red Zodiac and motored south to Lester's house, where Neil had the oxygen waiting. The tide was not all the way in, and we sometimes had to get out and walk the boat through the shallows for several hundred yards at a stretch. Landmarks went by, a downed drug plane, Autec Site 7 on High Point Cay, and finally the phone office at Mars Bay. We made it to within 60 ft (18 m) of the Hole before the prop guard scraped the sand. We towed it the last few yards to shore, and kitted up. Rob used the boat's anchor to rebelay the shotline, which we'd previously just attached to a rod in the sand 60 ft (18 m) down.

We left the oxygen tanks at 30 ft (9 m), and descended without incident to the lead weight on the shotline at −165 ft (−50 m). All our primary lights were working this time, but the visibility was less than on the previous dive – perhaps it was today's incoming tide, or even silt stirred up on our previous dive two days ago. We quickly made our way, breathing from our stage bottles, to the end of the line. There I changed valves, over to my 'hundreds', and was relieved to find that the second regulator, which had been giving some trouble on the surface, was now breathing smoothly. Rob tied off the spool and reeled on. I was spending a great deal of concentration on keeping tabs on every piece of gear, and playing out in my mind what I would do if he had a problem. It was very taxing. All of the usual narcosis symptoms were there, but all were familiar by now, and not frightening by themselves.

The depth gauge was now reading 260 ft (78 m), and I felt in control, though it seemed we were moving very slowly. That was good, actually, since heavy exertion at depth is the number one killer, undoubtedly what had got Dana Turner when he and Sheck Exley were working in Sally Ward

Hole in North Florida at −280 ft (−84 m), back in the early 1970s. I thought of all this while down there, of the very few cave divers that had ever penetrated this realm, and felt good in their presence. I had finally earned my diploma from my mentor, the master Exley, seven years after first deep-diving with him and wondering if I could ever go deeper than −235 ft (−70 m). Now of course helium had changed all the rules, and even Exley was using it. But to go to −260 ft (−78 m) on air was something of a personal accomplishment, even if records were not involved.

Rob soon tied off the line about 120 ft (36 m) beyond the previous limit of penetration. Ahead of him, in the dimness, we could see the floor rising again. I had been paying particular attention to the walls on the way in, following Rob, and had already come to the conclusion that this was probably nothing more than the edge of a large chamber that we were simply skirting round, and that no tunnel along the fault would be forthcoming. Rob must have recognized this also, for when he tied off the line he motioned me to wait and keep an eye on him. He dropped the spool on the floor, headed down some 10 ft (3 m) further, and stuck his hand in the bottom, going for maximum depth. We figured later that he had been roughly 270 ft (80 m) down. Both of us felt in control, and both later remarked about the mental strain of keeping everything in line at that depth. My feeling on the way to 265 ft (80 m) was that everything was going good, but that we were right there on the edge and a major problem would be touch and go. I could see now why Paul de Loach and John Zumrick, two of Florida's most experienced deep-cave divers, had mentioned being exhausted after their 260 ft (78 m) dive in 1975 at Wakulla Springs. John had said that it took him everything he had to survey out and stay level-headed.

When Rob returned, I surveyed out, while he provided light for me to read the compass and write on the slate. I felt very good with him as a partner. Very little had to be said or communicated for us both to understand perfectly what had to be done. I could ask for no better person to be with on the edge. Back on the shotline, we both made our way up to the 60 ft (18 m) stop, where I worked out that we needed to spend 30 minutes – sufficiently conservative, as we had oxygen for our 30 ft (9 m), 20 ft (6 m) and 10 ft (3 m) stops. Everything then got extremely boring for the following two and a half hours. The oxygen was in 104 cu. ft (9 cu. m) tanks, tremendously difficult to deal with; there was just no place to hang them off our harnesses without unbalancing the whole thing. Bits fell off in the struggle. So somewhere at the bottom of Mars Bay Blue Hole lies my new Casio watch.

Rob Palmer: While this was going on, Stuart, Neil and I bounced to 200 ft (60 m) on the rebreathers with no real difficulty at all, surfacing to a glorious red sunset lake one evening. Now things were really moving.

CHAPTER NINE

Elvenhome and El Dorado

W AY BACK in 1985, during the final days that Operation Raleigh spent on South Andros, it had become increasingly obvious that we were going to under-achieve terribly. We had one good discovery, Stargate, and little else except for a bunch of pretty-looking marine entrances and a few fairly minor inland caves. From maps and aerial photographs, we could see that there were entrances all over the place in the interior, many not too far from the road, but our utter lack of transport meant that few of these were going to be reached.

In the last few days I took Mark Vinall, one of the underwater photographers and a keen caver back home in the UK, aside and suggested we have a brief look at a series of entrances a little north of Stargate, behind the primary school at the northern end of the Bluff. We snuck off one day in late February, just the two of us and one set of diving gear, to see what lay up there.

School Hole, as we called the large blue hole immediately behind the school, was uninviting, and an appalling indictment of Bahamian environ-mental education. Behind the building, the ground was littered with old cans, broken glass, tattered exercise books and assorted debris that stretched down to the water's edge and beyond. The hole stank of urine and sulphur, and was surrounded by a ragged, broken fence of pig-wire, remnants of an effort by some concerned individual in the past to keep the kids out of the water. The size and shape of most of the holes in the wire showed what a useless attempt this had been – about as effective as the directive that was responsible for painting 'MOVE' in bright yellow paint on all the abandoned, rusting wrecks by the side of the road. From the school, a waste pipe led into the ground a few metres short of the water; it took little imagination to decide where the school sewage ended up.

Disgusted, we wandered south along an overgrown track to try and find the next entrance on the map. A rough side path, barely visible in places, took us to a long gash of an entrance, a deep narrow rift about 60 ft (18 m) long that fell vertically down to dark water. It was almost invisible from a few metres away, lurking secretively in deep jungle that clawed our bodies as we fought our way to the edge. It was the antithesis of School Hole; it was obvious that no one regarded this as a playground, it had an air of slight menace about it, and the sides looked far too steep for children to climb easily.

We brought my gear over from the road, slightly concerned at our lack of rope or ladder. Getting into the water in these caves was never a problem, gravity sucks, the only worry was missing the branches as we leapt from the edge. Normally, most Holes had a small gully or a rockfall up which one could clamber out, but this Hole was sheer-sided, and offered no easy exit. I looked optimistically at a rotting tree that hung down into the water.

'I reckon I'll be able to climb out on that tree.'

'You sure? What about the gear?' Mark was more dubious.

'Um, that probably won't be a problem. Maybe I can climb out with it on, or I could dekit in the water and try and slide it up first. You can probably get on that ledge and reach it, anyway.'

The ledge in question was a loose and dirty collection of rubble that teetered on a lip half-way down the east wall. Mark looked distinctly unenthusiastic. I scoffed at his lack of confidence.

But a few minutes later, teetering on the lip of the shaft, I felt a little less certain. Deciding that the embarrassment of a potential 'rescue' by the team back at Kemps Bay would spur me to regain the top, I took a couple of ungainly lurches in lieu of a run-up and crashed through the last yard or two of undergrowth like a neoprene-clad rhino, soaring in lumpen flight down the 20 ft (6 m) to the water. The walls echoed, birds rose screeching, and my mask came adrift.

Bobbing to the surface, I spat sulphurous water from my mouth, and grubbed at a lump of algal crud that hung disgustingly from the mouthpiece of one regulator. The waves splattered the walls, and diminished as the lake settled again. A large frog glared at me, croaking antagonistically.

'Bog off,' I croaked back, gagging on the sulphur and suddenly much less enthusiastic about the current situation. The water was brown, the walls sheer, and there felt nothing shallow about this place. A more oppressive diving site from water level I had yet to see.

Mark looked through the gap I had made in the jungle. I looked back, smiling as confidently as I could, hoping for a chance to delay things by making small talk.

'Get on with it, then. I'm being bloody eaten alive up here.'

Well on a par with Captain Oates, I thought. The supportive camaraderie and intuitive understanding of people who live on the edge is something the ordinary world barely dreams of.

'You going, or not?'

I muttered something about finding a belay for the line.

'Try the flake you're holding on to.'

Oh yes, *this* flake, just why I'd picked it, of course. I wrapped the line round it, and turned my lights on. I looked underwater. Absolutely dark. Alien. Anything could be in there. Luscas. Big slimy eels. Mark looked hopeful.

'See anything?' he asked cheerfully.

'Sort of a fine Keemun, perhaps a little steeped,' I replied, trying half-heartedly for what I imagined to be up-market humour.

'You what?' said Plymouth's version of *Homo neanderthalis*. Underwater suddenly began to have its attractions; I blew algae from my second stage, and stuck it in my mouth. Sulphur really does taste foul.

I stared at the wall all the way down to 60 ft (18 m). It gave a certain comfort and broke the monotony, every time I glanced the other way it simply looked dark and scared me. The walls were brown, and draped with sepulchral algae, a morbid reminder of decay. The mixing zone arrived, and things lost focus.

And shimmered back into cave. I hung over a Stargate void, shining walls soaring white and clear down to unfathomed depths. Tiny flecks of light in the water swam with fairy grace, taking lunch in the bottom-most layers of the organic soup above. I moved out into open water, leaving a trail of thin line behind, into a new world.

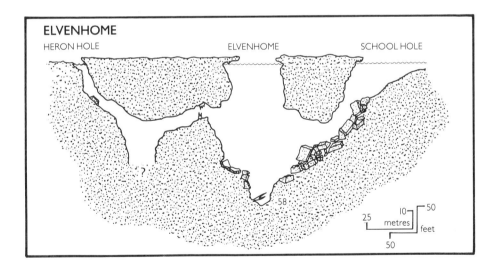

The passage through the dark mists had seemed like a departure from a world I knew into a new one, another dimension. This world was of dark space, hewn from the island by forces I knew little about, enclosed in a shell of limestone. In an alcove on the eastern wall, a group of gnarled, strangely twisted stalagmites hunched together like a gathering of dwarfs, bent over unseen work. The tiny cave animals that swam in the waters around seemed like delicate sprites flying in their ebony firmament. *Elvenhome,* I thought, that's the name for this cave. I moved slowly north along the deep abyss. Dimly, through the darkness below, I could make out a floor of huge boulders rising towards me out of the void. The main cave was shallow, much more so than Stargate, and I moved below the clouds of the halocline for most of the way.

Not that that was far. Only 100 ft (30 m) or so into the passage, I came across a massive choke of collapsed rubble, huge boulders poised one on another in arrested flight. I hung well back, and put a hand out to a ledge on the wall. On which was a book.

A little nonplussed, I suddenly realized that this choke must lie directly under School Hole. Looking more closely, several bits of debris amongst the choke turned out to be exercise books, plastic bags, and rusting drinks cans. A world-famous beer company proved that once again they were 'reaching the parts that other beers couldn't'. I tied the line off on the east wall, and swam back, unwilling to try and surface through the choke, and more unwilling to swim in the upper, polluted waters of School Hole.

Mark peered at me as I surfaced. Gasping for air that didn't taste of sulphur, I clung to the slimy tree that represented my escape route. It groaned sepulchrally and sank beneath my weight into the depths.

I looked round the walls. Another tree hung low over the water, growing from a ledge. I could pull up on that, and get to the ledge, and then to the top. Hampered by the weight of two 80 cu. ft (6.8 cu. m) air tanks, and a lead weightbelt, I hauled myself upwards. One foot, two feet on the wall, a metallic layback on the thorny tree. Six feet (1.8 m) up the wall, it rebelled. Clutching a branch in my hand, I hurtled backwards into the lake with a terrific splash. Mark hooted.

Floating in the water, eyeing possible routes up the wall, I did my best to ignore the helpful suggestions that came mockingly from above. In as level a voice as I could muster, I suggested Mark might usefully descend as far as the ledge, and try and help me out. He scrambled down, and looked at me, fighting hysteria.

I went for it. Muscles rippled as I hauled me and 80 lb (36 kg) of metal vertically up the wall on frictional holds. From a foot away, I glared triumphantly into Mark's face.

He looked at my fingers as they opened out in protest at the strain. I waved weakly as gravity reasserted itself.

'Bye, Rob,' he smirked, drowned by the splash.

About half an hour later, I staggered to the top of the cliff, having taken all my gear off in the water and half-climbed the rock many times to heave it at arm's length to Mark's outstretched hands. I was exhausted. We staggered back to the last-night party, me vowing never to dive Blue Holes again.

Richard hung in the clear water by the boulder choke below School Hole. A foot in front of his mask, a pale cave-fish rippled its fins and moved leisurely away, tired of the intrusion. The way down had been simple, an overhanging cavern at the surface had led vertically down to meet my two-year-old line, though my worst fears about the water quality of the Hole behind the school seemed justified (indeed they were – everyone who dived through it fell victim to a mysterious blood infection that brought with it large and painful septic sores, making diving a really unpleasant experience while they lasted).

Bill Stone and Rob Parker had, a few days earlier, taken the more orthodox entry into the system through the narrow gash of Elvenhome, and had reached bottom below the entrance at −190 ft (−57 m). I had been down to take a sediment sample, and the base of the cave was depressing, again sulphurous and silty, with rotting vegetation standing in skeletal disarray from the mung. Below 140 ft (42 m), the caves all seemed brown and depressing, more so if organic matter had a direct run at the water column.

South of Elvenhome, a trail wound for a few hundred metres to a third water surface, a small pool in the northern corner of a wide and overgrown collapse. Tall reeds and ferns fringed the water, and the glade that formed the entrance was more pleasant by far than the other two nearby. A grey heron, nesting in the reeds and disturbed by the intrusion, provided the name for the entrance, Heron Hole. Richard and I intended to connect all three entrances, if possible, and make an accurate map of the cave.

We photographed our way along to where a dim green glow in the water above told us we were below Elvenhome. Leaving the old line on the west wall, we swam across the passage to a ledge at −80 ft (−24 m), to tie on the new line. Richard took it, and I followed him with the camera, photographing his exploration of the southern canyon that led towards Heron Hole. The passage soon left the great entrance abyss behind, and rose almost into the mixing zone, as we swam over a col-like barrier of rock, decorated by a few dusky pillars. Over the other side, the floor fell steeply away again, and was soon lost in inky blackness below. We finned on between two enclosing walls, down the middle of the canyon towards a silt slope, where black, decaying branches and rotting leaves suggested we couldn't be far from daylight. I looked up at Richard, and saw him silhouetted in the tannic glow from Heron Hole, framed by dead trees and the harsh rock walls of the cave.

Surfacing only long enough to tie the line to the side and gasp in a few congratulatory breaths of fresh air, we returned the way we came, surveying along the line in the dark waters. Fragments of bacterial plate, broken from the roof by our bubbles, sank past us in the water, obscuring much of our vision. Fiona came down to meet us in Elvenhome, alerted to our return by the bubbles breaking surface. We set a line of tiny limestone pills in down the wall, to see what effect the change in water chemistry at increasing depth had on the rock, and set out through School Hole again. Decompressing in the polluted waters was not an experience I would particularly like to repeat. It was virtually impossible to read gauges at the shallowest stop, and the changes in temperature between differing chemical layers were abrupt and quite intense. We were all glad to get out, but we were also rather pleased at making a unique three-way link up between the different Blue Holes on the line.

Stargate lay behind the village of The Bluff, a long meandering settlement that was probably the largest of the South Andros communities. In the two years since we first visited it, new houses had crept nearer to the cave entrance, threatening its future existence as a cave and not a rubbish dump. The opening still lay through several hundred feet of scrub, along a small path that we trimmed back a little to give us access with the grand paraphernalia of deep-water cave exploration. The immediate surroundings of the entrance were cleared, removing the thin scrub that had grown since the slash-and-burn farmers had last passed this way. A simple awning was slung between trees to give some respite from the scorching sun, and several of the large Air Products gas tanks were carried over to provide breathing gas for the bail-out umbilical which now hung down the shaft.

Brad Pecel, one of the divemasters at Small Hope Bay who had flown down to help out for a few weeks, astounded everyone by simply picking up one of the large oxygen 'J' tanks, slinging it on one shoulder, and casually wandering off barefoot along the path while we others struggled to haul one there between two of us. Brad's strength had rapidly become a point of awe among the rest of us, and Rob Parker took this casual might like a personal affront. In turn, he staggered along the track with a big tank, strapped into a backpack like some over-enthusiastic SCUBA diver out for a good time. Brad, with genuine good nature, seemed oblivious to the admiration we had for his vitality and dedication to sheer hard work.

After a couple of days of hard work, things were virtually ready to go. A generator was started; the Compaq computer fired up to read out decompression profiles on site; cameras were ready to roll and two rebreathers were fully charged and lowered into the mouth of the cave. Stuart and I stood on a scaffolding gantry erected in the entrance to Stargate, and swung down into the water. A couple of days before, I had been down briefly below the entrance to 230 ft (70 m) on air SCUBA, and could see no way on below. We were worried that the cave might be bottoming out too soon.

The plan was complicated. Stuart and I were using the units for the first time in a real cave, but because of the delays in the schedule, we were also going to try for a work dive, and collect some deep stalagmite samples. Additionally, because of their own compressed schedule, our National Geographic film crew were also going to try and get some film in the can. We planned a tightly scheduled dive, with deliberate sequences for the camera, and a strict timetable for descent and work. Off we all went, down the shotline, and into the South Passage. There, the problems started.

As we sank through the mixing zone into the clear waters of the great entrance chasm, the filming lights blazed on. Dazzled, I turned the switch on the 250-watt light I carried strapped below the Acurex bail-out tank on my chest. Nothing happened. I shook the pack, and twisted the switch again, but the unit stayed resolutely off. This meant I had nothing to fight the film lights back with. I swam south into a blinding azure haze, more than slightly disorientated, and hoping I was in the centre of the canyon. The lights dimmed for a moment as I swam into the south passage, and I gestured frantically at Paul Atkins, behind the camera. He was oblivious to my problem and was getting irritated, assuming I was simply not following the schedule we'd worked out on the surface. I continued as best I could, hoping he could catch something from the changing conditions. At a rock ledge on the east wall, at -120 ft $(-36\,\text{m})$, I tied a new line reel on and began to descend, still blinded by the lights. I was moving off course, away from the centre of the cave, without realizing it. A torch on my helmet brushed the tip of a large pear-shaped stalactite. The finely tuned crystal snapped, and 40 lb (18 kg) of white calcite slammed into me from above, a pure white spear that pierced the shoulder of my drysuit like a lance. Snapping sideways, the heavy crystal pillar jammed across the top of my rebreather.

It felt as though the roof had fallen in. Without any idea of what was going on, I was suddenly tumbling backwards, swept almost upside-down. I began falling deeper into the cave. Frantically squirting air into my drysuit, I waved at Stuart, trying to suggest he might like to save my life. He looked blankly at me, wondering what on earth was going on. It seemed an age (though it must have been seconds) before he moved in, and grabbed the pillar. I reorientated myself, and turned to see him swimming heavily away with his arms full of stalactite, looking for a ledge to dump it on while I composed myself. Unaware of a calcite plug in my shoulder, where the tip of the pillar had wedged itself, I was for continuing the dive. Stuart waved an emphatic no, and pointed me out, knocking my hand from my shoulder when I felt to check. Unsure of his meaning, I felt a sudden surge of fear. Had the stalactite torn the breathing hose? The only real worry with the rebreathers was just that very thing; if water got into the system in large quantities through a broken hose then the breathing gas would be suddenly replaced by a toxic surge of soda lime cocktail, a lethal mixture that would burn lungs out almost instantly.

I grabbed at the regulator on the emergency tack and stared at Stuart questioningly. Apprehension must have burnt like a halo round me. Stuart shook his head, and waved a negation. I waved the regulator again. I have no interest in hot lungs. Stuart waved a negative, then gave the OK sign, knocked my nervous hand away from my shoulder once again, and gestured emphatically out.

We gained the shotline, and rose gradually to our first decompression stop. Because the plan had been suddenly broken, our precisely planned dive profile now had to be recalculated, and a new decompression schedule worked out. The divers with the rebreathers had to be perfectly timetabled – even the speed of descent was crucial, and any variation from the plan meant that the special decompression profiles must be changed to suit. That was why we had a computer on the surface above. With the tables logged in its memory, it could respond quickly to a change in the programme, and work out a revised set of times with lightning speed while the divers waited below.

On the surface, Yanto and Bill were sitting by the pool, acting as dive marshalls. Yanto was looking at the hideously complicated form that controlled the operation, giving an exact depth and location for the planned dive that they all assumed was taking place below.

'What depth are they at now, Yanto?' asked John Mylroie, one of the geologists.

'Two hundred and thirty feet,' replied Yanto, looking at the form and his stopwatch. He looked at Bill, and they grinned, secure that all was going happily as planned.

Brad surfaced. 'We've got an abort.'

Bill looked at Yanto with a what-happens-next look. Yanto looked back with his best I-don't-know-I've-never-done-this-job-before eyes. Brad passed his slate up through several pairs of hands to Yanto, while down below, at 140 ft (42 m), Stuart and I hung on the line, waiting for the umbilical to be switched on.

Bill's hands flickered at the computer keyboard. A new set of tables was compared with the old, and it was decided, as no one yet knew exactly what had happened, that an extended decompression might not be a bad idea. A brief message to this effect was scrawled on Brad's slate, and he disappeared in a welter of bubbles, tracking back down the line to us with the revised schedule.

The umbilical was switched on, as an emergency bailout should something further happen, and Stuart grabbed the mouthpieces as we rose to the 70 ft (21 m) mark, trailing them with us as we rose from stop to stop.

Our dive had been brief. We were soon at 40 ft (12 m), changing over from the rebreathers to the umbilical set piping pure oxygen down for the final stretch. Though the rebreather itself would deliver pure oxygen at these shallowest stops, a switch to 'open-circuit' oxygen meant that even the trace amounts of helium in our exhaled breath were exhausted from the system, instead of passing round the rebreather to be inhaled again. Everything we could do to reduce the possiblity of decompression sickness was a bonus. As the inert gas came out of solution in our tissues, it was purged from our bodies, and we could ascend with safety to the surface.

At the gantry, Stuart reached over and, with a grin, plucked the calcite fragment out of the hole in my shoulder. Air gushed from my suit, and I

Keith Turner and Paul Atkins film the preparations for the day's deep dive. Bill
Hamilton gives computer predictions to Stuart and Rob Parker while Sharon
Yskamp notes details. *(Photo: Rob Palmer)*

grabbed hurriedly at the scaffolding to stop myself from sinking into the
depths again. A memorable first dive!

On the surface, I dekitted thoughtfully, taking a long pull at the water
flask. Paradoxically, I was safer on the rebreather than I would have been
on SCUBA gear. The worst that could have happened would have been a long
rock-climb back to the surface from the bottom of the cave; there had been
little likelihood that I would have run out of breathing gas. Our portable
Compaq computer on the surface would have given Bill Hamilton the
chance to recompute our decompression schedule on site, and though we
might have spent several hours extra in the water, I would probably have
lived through the experience. Life still felt pretty fragile for an hour or so,
though. It had been an interesting first trip for the rebreathers.

And, as it turned out, my last. Bill was getting fairly uptight about the
possibility that he might not be able to use the units. Though he had been
part of the original line-up, he'd missed out on the training programme at
Fort Bovisand and the compressed schedule made it seem that his chances
of being trained in the field were receding fast. For someone so involved
with rebreather research, it was becoming unacceptable for him to stand on
the sidelines. His diary records his thoughts.

I am concerned about Palmer's identifying himself and Parker as the two
prime divers to use the close-circuit rigs. The understanding had always

been in my mind that all three of us would be using them. It smacked of nationalism, and I for one would not forgive that kind of behaviour. Obviously this is Palmer's expedition, and ethically I could not do anything to impede it. I have discussed the matter with him, but he seems not to grasp the gravity of the situation.

In fact, I understood the situation perfectly, and sympathized greatly with Bill. But the safe success of the whole programme was greater than the ego of any individual team member. Rob Parker and I talked it over, after Rob had offered to drop out and offer Bill his place. Though it was a noble gesture, the problem went deeper than simple nobility.

Basically, we would work more efficiently on the rebreather dives with two established teams of two. This meant that one of the three of us had to drop out. Stuart had a voice in matters as well, it was his equipment, and his company's reputation at stake if anything went wrong. Bill's lack of prior training might seriously slow the programme again at this stage, but his innate ability and great theoretical knowledge would probably balance out his lack of practical experience. After much heart-searching, and a couple of late nights gazing at the stars with a can of beer, the solution seemed obvious.

Bill would go on the rebreathers, and team up with Neil as the main scientific team. Rob and Stuart would work on the film, and add to the scientific collection when circumstance allowed. I would come off the rebreathers, and work on open-circuit deep dives at other sites in support of Pete's scientific programme. This was the best solution. Bill's future research would undoubtedly benefit, his morale would improve generally, and he had worked hard to earn his place. Rob had a lot of experience at working with film crews, and would do that job well. I was better than he was at scientific work, and had more interest in it, and otherwise had no better reason to be on the rebreathers than the other two, save that I'd spent a long time setting up the project, and would be as disappointed as either of them at missing the cream from the cake. Anyway, it would give me a chance to look around more, and do some exciting diving. I persuaded myself I wouldn't suffer much.

Bill: Palmer arrived at about 6.45 am and we discussed the course of the deep diving. He explained that, to satisfy all the parties involved, film, geology, deep diving and survey work, I would take Parker's place on the deep diving project, Parker would take his place on the underwater film work, and he would assist Pete Smart with the science work, deep-diving on air. Now, this was all well and good, and meant that I would finally have a chance to get some working time on the rebreather. But the way he presented it, I was made to feel that he was getting the bum end of the deal. In my mind there should have been no problem, with a friendly rotation, between himself, Parker and me regarding the deep work. The problem, of course, was that Carmellan had absolute control over the actual use of the rebreathers, as well they should, since they owned them, but there were only two of them and three of us. And both Robs had had prior chamber work in Britain, which in some sense made them more fit. If one looked to the future, however, then my getting experience on the rigs in real diving situations would have a much more long-range payback to the cave-diving community, since this hands-on practical experience would help in the design of the new cave-diving rebreather I was working on in Washington.

Now I hand it to Palmer for being a gentleman about the matter; he certainly has put an awful lot of work into making all this happen. But I feel he has made the classic two mistakes that many expedition leaders, myself included, make – too large a team, which makes it difficult to manage and co-ordinate; and plans of action which are too difficult to focus the team as a whole on. The focus is really the main thing, and here on Andros, even after all the hassels of the start-up phase, which in reality all expeditions have, and which all must suffer through until things run smoothly, it was difficult to put a finger on what the expedition objective was. After thinking about it a while, I realized that most of the projects I have run have done best when there has been a solitary objective, the path to which has been dead clear to nearly every member of the team.

Rob Palmer: Bill, I guess, was right, to a degree. The Andros Project was many things to many people, and it is hard to blame individuals for jostling for position when they feel their aspect of the fieldwork is in jeopardy. By making my choice the way I did, I feel I did my best to draw the focus back into perspective, and add a little more direction to the deep-diving work. We were not there simply to see how the rebreathers worked in caves; we were there to do practical work with them. If simplifying the rebreather teams helped that, then it was important that that was done. Sensibly, there was no real room for an aquatic game of 'musical chairs' just to let everyone play with the systems in the water. I hid my disappointment by looking for new challenges elsewhere, in between the scientific work with Pete, and the logistical headaches that each new day seemed guaranteed to drag out of nowhere.

CHAPTER TEN

El Dorado and beyond the limits of Stargate

I N THE autumn of the year before, 1986, following our reconnaissance, hints of an American visit to South Andros had begun to filter through on the grapevine. When a more accurate tale came from Bill Stone, I was pretty bemused. Dennis Williams, a Grand Bahama resident and a very experienced cave diver whom we had invited to join the 1987 team, had decided that he did not want to share any biological glory that might be had with our other cave biologist, Tom Iliffe from Bermuda, and had snuck in first, without telling us.

I had no real problems with such a visit, other than the manner in which it was conducted. It emerged that Dennis and Tom had fallen out during a small biological expedition to the Pacific, but rather than discuss this with me, and see how one or both might still be able to work on Andros, Dennis had decided simply to move in with three other divers and, in the words of one quote that reached us, 'leave nothing left to explore'.

This was all a bit pathetic. If he had had the courtesy to have contacted us, something could have been easily worked out to suit all concerned. I'd worked with Dennis before on Grand Bahama, and had always passed details of any of our Bahamian work on to him, a favour that was not always reciprocated. I suspect Dennis tended to regard the Bahamas as his own personal territory, and still saw us as interlopers, despite the fact that we had probably explored more sites than he had, and had certainly made much more of an effort to share our discoveries responsibly with the rest of the world. Some people are like that, seeing discovery in personal terms, and part of Dennis's excuse was that he felt that these places should be kept secret, to avoid human interference. I can sympathize with that, but only to a certain extent, for it sometimes means that they suffer because no one knows they are there. However, Dennis never seemed to be averse to publicizing his own work when there was some personal benefit to be had.

The other three divers were probably oblivious to all the 'political background', and I couldn't blame them any. Dennis is one of the glibbest, silver-tongued characters on the cave-diving scene, and Andros is an exciting place. I had little doubt that we had been convincingly presented as trans-Atlantic poachers. That the entire purpose behind the Andros Project was to bring those who had been working on Blue Holes on both sides of the Atlantic together seemed irrelevant to Dennis.

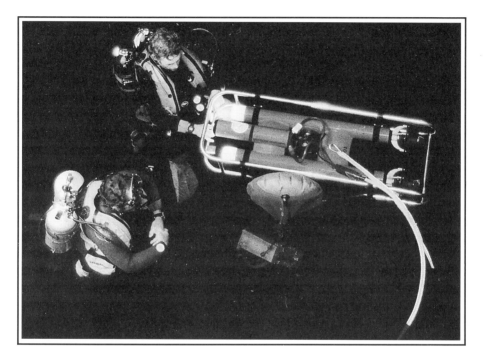

Paul Atkins and Keith Turner manoeuvre the Phantom ROV on the surface of Stargate. *(Photo: Chris Howes FRPS)*

Project Andros, as Dennis called his small expedition, spent a lot of time going where we had been before, and their report in one of the American cave-diving magazines caused some amusement among our team on Andros. Oblique references were made to the fact that someone else had been in the caves, but no real credit was given to any of the work we had done. Stargate they enthused greatly about, and they had explored a little further down South Passage than my solo limit in 1985. They 'rediscovered' Jellyfish Lake, and renamed it 'Swimming Hole', and there one of the divers, Parker Turner, managed to pass a horrific squeeze. Using a single tank, he passed through a narrow crack between two boulders at the northern end of the cave, and entered a complex series of rifts which became too tight for further progress after 200 ft (60 m). In one of these rifts, he made an exciting discovery. Down one wall, cascading on to ledge after ledge, a wealth of tiny fossilized bones poked from the fine silt. Minute jawbones, little long-bones, ribs and skulls revealed them to be *hutia*, a large rodent now extinct in the Bahamas on all but a few uninhabited cays in the Exumas. Their fragile nature, and the depths at which they were found, suggested that they had been underwater for a long time, perhaps several thousand years. It appeared to be the remains of an ancient nesting site, perhaps of one of the extinct giant barn owls – the Chickcharnie of Androsian mythology, and this cascade of bones represented the remains of hundreds of predatorial meals in ancient days, before the seas had fully risen to flood the shallowest levels of the caves.

The main discoveries of the Americans had been in the two blue holes further north of Jellyfish Lake/Swimming Hole. One, the first, was a smallish pool about 60 ft (18 m) in diameter, with a 15 ft (4.5 m) vertical cliffs down to water level, but the next one along was huge, about 300 ft (90 m) long. Cliffs at the southern end gave way to an immense chaotic boulder collapse at the northern extreme, where jungle-covered slabs led right down to the water's edge. Half-way along the lake, the floor rose up from its southern depths to a shallow, sandy underwater beach, covered in algal gardens like those of Evelyn Green's and Gopher Hole. It was a beautiful place, open, sunny, and full of life.

At the northern end of this lake, across the boulder slopes, a dark rift led into the side of an ancient fossil dune, where drifting sand had long since turned to rock. The great fracture cut through the ancient dune, and for once the cave passages did not lie underwater. The Americans had explored Rat Bat Cave, named after the hundreds of little furry animals hanging from the roof, through to the fourth Blue Hole in the series. Pools in the floor of the cave connected together underwater, in a short series of dives. To get there dry involved a constricted squeeze near water level, beneath a ledge on which, in 1987, a sizeable boa constrictor had made its bed.

The centre Hole, between Jellyfish Lake and Rat Bat Lake, they called El Dorado. An underwater connection was made between El Dorado and Rat Bat Lake, the first major traverse of two Blue Hole entrances on Andros, but the plum lay in the other direction. Mike Madden and Parker Turner swam down the southern continuation of the connecting cave, through what Dennis had described as a 'Volkswagen-sized squeeze' (and which Mike, the first through it, called 'Puerto del Diablo' – the Devil's Doorway) into the roof of a mind-blowing abyss. Hanging on the roof at 240 ft (72 m), Parker lowered a shotline into the void. They estimated the point at which the line hit rock to be somewhere near 290 ft (87 m). This tremendous discovery was somewhat tempered by a rather arrogant quote in their report – 'I'd like to see them walk on the bottom in that place!'

Such sarcasm was a red flag to a bull. Bill and I filled two of the Acurex tanks with heliox, and made a plan. Bill, now on the rebreather project, was unable to dive to any great depth in view of the fact he was committed to a deep dive in Stargate the following day. I now had no such limitations. Bill would come in and support me to a depth of about 180 ft (54 m) and cover me in case anything happened on the ascent. El Dorado was a long way further into the bush than any of the deep sites we had so far worked, and would therefore be a very committing dive. It would also take a bit more in the way of gear hauling to reach the site.

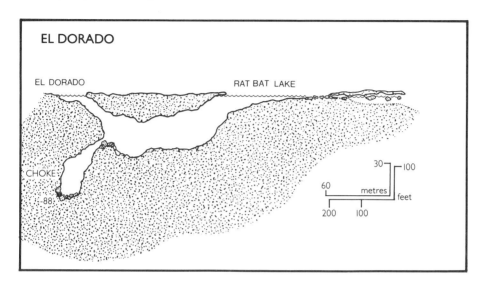

Bill Stone pumps a heliox mix into a lightweight Acurex cylinder, using the boxed Haskel Booster Pump. *(Photo: Rob Palmer)*

The jungle north of Congo Town, in which the northern series of caves lie, is more primeval than almost anywhere else in the Bahamas. It seems to have escaped the 'slash-and-burn' approach to farming, and as a result is often easier to move through, the well-developed overstory keeping under-growth to a minimum. But where daylight enters, and the high woods thin out, it can be as dense as anything the coastal strip has to offer. Hauling double backpacks and diving gear for a mile or more through it, even with the aid of machetes to open up overgrown trails and to trim encroaching cactus, was desperately hot, back-breaking toil.

The struggle into gear in the bush at the top of the Hole was similarly appalling. I intended to use a drysuit and a bouyancy vest, to provide added safety in case one system ruptured. I had just had a close shave in Stargate, and was only too aware of the lethal consequences of trying to walk back out along the bottom of El Dorado, at nearly 300 ft (90 m) on SCUBA gear. I would be breathing from two side-mounted Acurex tanks full of air on the descent, and carrying a third Acurex on my chest with a 20 per cent oxygen/80 per cent helium mix for the deep stuff. There was no way this lot could be put on above water; I would have succumbed to heatstroke long before hitting the Hole.

Even in the lake things were little easier. The extra buoyancy of the Acurex tanks and the distribution of additional lead around my body did not quite mesh – I felt unwieldy and out of tune. Vocally, I pulled at straps and changed weights, trying to swear everything more evenly in place. Out of the water I would have weighed about 250 lb (112.5 kg) in all this gear. The heliox tank on my chest tank kept riding up and blocking my view, bouyant even with a heavy 250-watt light slung beneath it. I felt my temper slipping, and frustration rising to an intolerable degree. I was on the point of calling off the dive.

A cry came from across the lake, telling us that the oxygen tanks had been set on a shotline. Short on breath and temper beneath the load, I dog-paddled across the lake with Bill. I hung by the wall, gasping for breath, and forcing myself to calm down.

'Let's do it' came a muffled grunt that Bill didn't hear. I clutched the reel, deflated the small amount of excess air from my suit, and sank into sulphurous gloom. Tiny jellyfish and strands of bacteria floated past, and I felt better with each passing moment. Bill, left on the surface looking at a small column of rising bubbles, decided he had probably better follow. The oxygen tanks came into view, and I looped the guideline round the shotcord to ensure that we could find them immediately. Behind, in the dull green gloom, the eastern wall of the cave showed vaguely through the twilight. I swam to it and continued on down, the wall providing the only reference point in the cloudy waters as the darkness enveloped us.

Sixty feet down, the cave came back. The water shimmered, and Bill and I emerged into clarity, suspended almost 100 ft (30 m) above the floor. The cave was dramatically different from Stargate. Few stalactites graced the walls, and everything was darker, more starkly defined. A gin-clear canyon headed north beyond the beam of our lights, towards Rat Bat, 500 ft (150 m) away. Across the passage a narrow rift led east. I went into it, knowing that the American passage went off generally in that direction, but the walls pinched in, and it closed down to nothing, a dead end. We backed out and turned south in the main cave, and there was the thin American line, running over a couple of black, rotting branches on the floor. Ahead lay Dennis's 'Volkswagen Squeeze', El Puerto del Diablo. I paralleled the American line, running my reel along the western wall to avoid entanglements. Down, hanging east round a corner, and out into the biggest, most gobsmacking hall I'd ever seen, the underwater Grand Canyon. The floor disappeared in a chaos of blocks and debris, tumbling into nowhere. Bill hung behind me and above me as I swam on beneath the rapidly descending roof, looking for the end of the other line. I switched on the 250-watt beam. Faint outlines of rocks could be seen far below. The Decobrain flickered figures, 200 ft (60 m), 220 ft (66 m). Ahead, the roof seemed to fall steeply down a pile of boulders. Below, darkness. This seemed to be it.

The slight narcosis of air added to the sense of wonder, of disbelief at the sheer size of the place. I checked the yellow heliox valve, purging a stream of bubbles that floated, saucer-like, wobbling towards the roof. I changed mouthpieces, air-red to heliox-yellow, and sucked in deeply. Three long, slow breaths, and my head cleared, as if by magic. None of the wonder went.

Bill hung several metres above, watching me change to heliox, spreadeagle my arms in an exhilarated mock-skydive, wave 'Here I go', and soar silently off. Bubbles crashed in silver streams from my regulator, rising in a shining cascade towards the roof far above. Bill had a grandstand view of one of the more dramatic moments of cave-diving exploration, a deep, remote penetration in one of the most spectacular underwater caves on Earth, breathing mixed gas beneath countless tons of solid rock, topped by a layer of prime Bahamian jungle.

I came to a rest a couple of feet above the floor. The reading on the Decobrain said 279 ft (85 m), and the cave still went down, curving under a ledge, though now much smaller, weaving down the wall beside the choked floor. With some pleasure, I laid a fin on the rocks.

Walked it, I thought, smugly.

I peered up at Bill's light, shining above me like a distant nova in a midnight sky. There was no simple belay for the line, so I moved carefully down, into a constricted, spiralling tunnel off the east side of the main cave. At −285 ft (−85 m), it grew too tight, a sharp-walled tube that led back towards the choke in the floor of the main chamber. I tried for a sample of the fine, light-brown sediment that covered the floor in front of my mask, but the cave was too constricted for me to be able to reach the pocket the plastic sample bags were in. Good British-type cave this bit, I thought, narrow, muddy and confining. I backed out. A low passage led off to one side, but far too tight for the amount of gear I bore. Below, the cave choked firmly.

I turned, and rose through the swirling silt to the main cave, pausing to tie the line off on a large slab. As I did so, a coil ran behind one of my tanks, catching on a hidden snag. I couldn't twist round to free it, its knotted loops were just out of finger reach at full stretch. Normally, this would be a potentially serious problem – and could have been lethal had I been breathing air – but on heliox with so much adrenalin flowing in my blood, and so much splendour around me, I found it hard to worry about it. I brought my knife out and casually cut the loop away. That done, and the line tied off, the chance of swimming free in the big hall was just too enticing. Off I went.

The utter thrill of hanging there, in the centre of that amazing cave, was immeasurable. It was beyond any dream of flight, for I was awake, aware. I floated, suspended, out of time and space. The cave swept on beyond, and it seemed I looked across aeons into an ageless night. Weightless, gravity had no hold on me. I cast a thought, breathe in, and I rise. Another thought, breathe out, and I sink. This is magical. This is truly real. Far in front, I could see the cave dividing, my passage turning away from the main route, which fell away across a boulder ridge into space. There was still a chance to go deeper in, further on.

But my timestream and the cave's are different. I am a finite creature and my life supply is running out. I think of a turn, move in the water, and see Bill across an infinite distance. I think of flying, and move towards him, the wings on my feet take me there. We make 'OK's, finger and thumb joining in a circle. He turns, and I follow him, towards the other dimension, back through the mists between.

The walls hold no obvious stalactites, but Bill points to an old weathered run of flowstone. This place is ancient. A few metres above, a run of organic debris holds another surprise – a morbid reminder of time. A broken, human thighbone protrudes from the mung. The hip joint is there, but the bone is broken above the knee. A rib lies beneath, but a short scout round reveals no other fragments, they must lie beneath the mung. The bone is stained, brown and etched. A drowned swimmer a decade ago? An escaped slave two centuries past? Or an ancient Arawak, some five hundred years or more gone? Who knows. Maybe next dive we'll photograph it, and collect it. For now, it gets left.

Bill is silhouetted against the entrance above. From here, the mists are brown and clear, looking out between the dimensions seems to be different, a clearer vision. The edge of the cave is black; Bill and his stream of air stand sharply within the skeletal remains of fallen trees, stark branches that reach with hooked fingers from a graveyard of silt. It is an eerie sight. The dream shimmers as I rise, moving slowly towards the outline of the decompression tanks above. Bill is there before me, and the sharp medical taste of the oxygen is a sudden contrast to the cold heliox. A long time passes. The stops ascend, and eventually Bill disappears, leaving me alone. My fins bite, cutting circulation, and I remove both them and my helmet. I try to doze. For safety's sake, I increase my last two stops by a factor of two, doubling the time the Decobrain suggests. Each inward breath of oxygen goes out with an added load of helium as my tissues disgorge the gas. At last, two hours and more after the dive began, I surface and swim back through the jellyfish to the ladder and the insect-bitten group above. The kit comes off, and I climb the rocky slope back to reality.

I can't resist a brief grin of triumph. I suck a breath or two of heliox and gabble in distorted Donald Duck tremelo.

'Gotta get back in there soon, hey?'

On the same day, Rob Parker and Stuart were diving in Stargate with the rebreathers. Before moving sideways into the passages to search for depth, they had one last attempt directly below the entrance to the cave. We had had conflicting opinions on this spot – Fiona swore she had plumbed it to 300 ft (90 m) with her salinity probe, but I'd dived it alone on air earlier in the trip, and found the thick rope shotline we hung down it lying in coils on a floor at −230 ft (−70 m). Rock walls rose all around, there seemed to be one way further down, but the lack of debris on the rocks had made me slightly suspicious. But a few days later Stuart and Neil descended to −150 ft (−45 m) and shone one of the big lights down. They too could see the coils below, and were also of the opinion that that was it.

But I had been breathing air, and at 230 ft (70 m) narcosis tends to limit horizons. The cave at that depth was dark and somewhat gloomy, it would have been easy to miss a shallower continuation, and I had not been sure of the west wall for some of the descent. I might just have ended up in a blind pocket to the east side. Neither Stuart nor Neil would swear to the west wall being there when they looked, so it seemed worth a more intelligible look with the rebreathers.

Descending straight down from the scaffolding platform, Stuart and Rob followed the white line of the nylon rope into the abyss. At −230 ft (−70 m), they came across the coiled end of the shotline on the ledge, but a few feet higher the wall on the west side opened out into a further shaft. The ledge was in a blind pocket, an enclosed hole from within which my narrowed narcotic perspective had not seen the higher parallel continuation.

They heaved the rope over into the new shaft, and followed it down. For Rob, still relatively new to the rebreathers, the silence was peculiar, no reassuring sound of bubbles crashing from the regulators exhaust, simply the muted tones of his own breathing, and an occasional click from the backpack as the sensors opened the solenoid and more oxygen entered the system. The sensor gauge would have read a slightly higher oxygen content as they descended, eased as they paused by an extra manual injection of helium to speed the balance up.

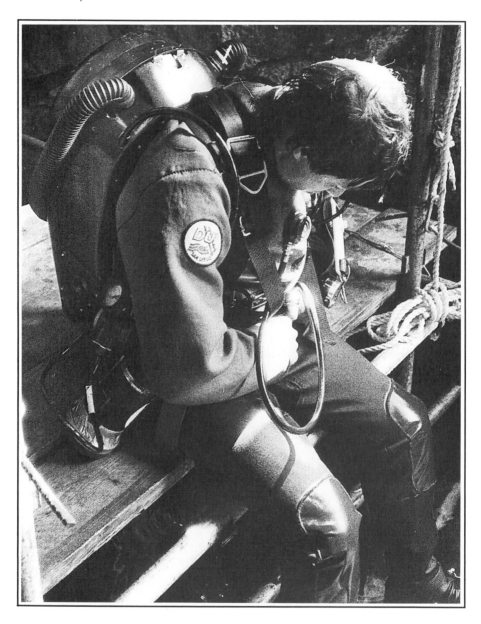

Rob Parker on the platform in Stargate, making final adjustments to the rebreather. *(Photo: Rob Palmer)*

The cave grew darker, the walls obscured by a thin film of brown sediment, the small ledges covered by decaying litter from above. At −300 ft (−90 m), they could see the outline of the bottom, a thick layer of detritus – broken branches, rotting leaves, bacterial mung – choking the now narrow cleft. Three hundred and twenty feet (96 m) below the surface, Rob thrust an arm into the short ruin, and thus 'bottomed' Stargate.

To say the least, we were disappointed. We had been on 'dry dives' to

500 ft (150 m) in the recompression chamber at Fort Bovistand, and hoped
to hit at least that in the caves. Despite the considerable achievement of
using mixed-gas rebreathers successfully in this remote field location, we
still hoped for the thrill of deep exploration to justify their potential fully.
Would moving away from the entrance, into the passages north or south,
reveal any greater depths? That was the next step – and before committing
the rebreather divers to a long horizontal swim if the system failed, we made
a preliminary reconnaisance on air.

In 1985 I had reached a point 500 ft (150 m) into the South Passage,
passing through a narrow gap at the apparent end into a large and rather
loose-looking chamber. The floor of the cave just before the squeeze had
been 200 ft (60 m) deep, a chaotic arrangement of boulders jammed across a
still-wide passage. The cave obviously continued beneath this, but for how
far? And would there by a way through the rocks?

The autumn before, the American team had been a little further into the
South Passage than I had. I had left the line tied to a large boulder next to
the narrow gap, having rewound the line that I had laid into the large
chamber beyond. Mike Madden tied his reel to my belay, and continued
with Roger Werner into the large boulder chamber, swimming across it for
200 ft (60 m) before encountering an enormous, multi-level boulder choke.
Though excited at the thought that they had 'broken Stargate open', they
took time out to begin the exploration of El Dorado. They understandably
became totally absorbed in this, and the connection through to Rat Bat
Lake, returning to Stargate only during the last days of their visit.

Mike and Roger entered the boulder choke at a depth of 180 ft (54 m),
where Roger's lights revealed a deeper continuation at 190 ft (57 m). At
210 ft (63 m), the way on was again in a jumble of breakdown, and they
ended their dive at this point. On their return, they collected tiny
crustaceans from the shallower waters above 150 ft (45 m), as part of
Dennis's biological survey. One of these turned out to be quite significant,
an amphipod much larger than any found previously in the caves.

Richard and I checked out the new extension to the South Passage fairly
early on, before the 320 ft (96 m) dive below the entrance. We used a single
'stage tank', and aluminium 80 cu. ft (6.8 cu. m) cylinder strapped to our
chests in addition to the two strapped to our sides. We left these at the
'squeeze', and passed through into the large chamber beyond.

Richard hung at 160 ft (48 m), while I dropped into the darkness at the
bottom of the chamber, 50 ft (15 m) or so before the final boulder choke.
From 200 ft (60 m) down, I found myself spiralling past giant boulders,
wedged precariously on steep slopes above the still-descending cave. By the
time I reached a depth of 250 ft (75 m), I could make out a floor of boulders
20 ft (6 m) below, in which dark holes led even deeper. On the edge of
narcosis, to descend further alone was ill-advised. I left the line reel on a
sloping boulder and, with a slow look round, rose through the darkness
towards Richard's lights far above.

At 250 ft (75 m), the dive computer on my arm told me my first 'stop' would be at −60 ft (−18 m), but the long swim out at about 100 ft (30 m), pausing to clip on the stage tanks en route, obviously served to clear much of my decompression time. By the time I reached the shotline under the entrance, the Decobrain was clearing me for a straight but slow ascent to 40 ft (12 m), though I still had to pay a further 109 minutes of dues before I could breathe fresh air again at the surface. I used the time to swim the circumference of the shaft at each successive stop, exploring the fossil coral reef that formed the walls of the shallowest cave, a stone record of the age before the Bahamas last rose above the waves to form the scattered islands of today. Sarah Cunliffe fell past us with Bish and Yanto in tow, in the final half-hour, 'bouncing' to 130 ft (40 m) to give Sarah and Yanto their first sight of the cave. Like everyone who entered Stargate for the first time, they emerged bubbling with enthusiasm for the place.

Having established that the far south of Stargate seemed to be going deep, Rob and Stuart and Neil and Bill started working their way along there, filming and collecting stalagmites for Pete Smart. Rob and Stuart claimed to have reached the end, and found no way on beyond their reel. Bill decided to have a run along on open-circuit heliox in SCUBA tanks to survey the cave, and try and find some way through. He set his oxygen decompression tank while Rob and Stuart completed a filming dive with the rebreathers, and made his dive as they surfaced.

Bill: I was feeling good about this dive . . . familiar with all the feelings. I could feel Exley and seven years of experience behind me. At −250 ft (−75 m), I could see Rob Parker's line reel sitting on top of a 20 ft (6 m)-high pinnacle of rock perched on one side of a tremendous chamber which dropped down and towards the west. I was puzzled. Rob and Stuart had said that the reel was on the bottom and there was no way on. Yet I could see 300 ft (90 m) and more in the gulf below where the reel was tied off. I took this in for a while, pondering whether or not to go for the depth – it did not look like there was any continuing passage down there, save for a small black spot in the boulders – or to pick up the reel and head south. I felt the price for depth too great, and decided to map what I could. I was still on air at this point and did not feel very bad, but nonetheless kept an instant eye on where the stage bottle regulator was located for quick access . . . salvation in the form of heliox.

I untied the reel and, prior to heading south, switched to the stage bottle. As Palmer had described in El Dorado, it took about three breaths for the helium to do its stuff. Magically, my head was clear and I was heading off into the unknown at −250 ft (−75 m). The wall that Parker and Stuart had described turned out to be a sloping breakdown pile. I reached a point some 150 ft (45 m) from the previous limit of exploration, and there found Palmer's reel on the breakdown. He had told me I might run into it, and had asked me to please collect it. I first went about a rebelay for my own line. There was about 0.5 in (1.27 cm) of silt on the rock and so a cloud soon enveloped me as I went about doing the tie-off. During this time I had set the reel down, and soon enough, quite to my surprise, I heard the unmistakable clang of the reel . . . some distance below me. I finished tying off the line, and when the silt settled I found the cord dropping down into a 3 ft (0.9 m) diameter hole in the breakdown. I started pulling the line out, in the hopes that it might have wrapped around the reel, but no such luck. The line just kept coming and coming. It was a no-win scenario, and I was glad I was on helium. Piles of floating line like this could easily be the end of a narked diver. I took a glance at the stage bottle gauge, and saw it to be near 'thirds'. At this point I still had to survey out, and had to reach the shotline before any changeover could be made back to air.

I collected Palmer's reel, abandoned the original reel as a lost cause, and began to survey out. It was about this time that it became apparent that the Acurex stage bottle was going buoyant. It rode up my left side, and started tipping me over. It was now a hassle to keep straight for the survey . . . and more gas was being used up. I could see by the 200 ft (60 m) mark that it was going to be close on the heliox. I really bombed out once the last survey reading was taken, and was soon at the 70 ft (20 m) decompression stop.

There was a momentary shake when I thought my decompression tables had somehow gone for the deep six after reclipping my dive-light. Fortunately they had caught on my harness, and floated in front of my mask. It would have been doubly embarrassing to have lost the large reel *and* got bent, having lost the deco tables too. This cave simply ate hardware. I paid some two hours' decompression for this little venture, and the only novel thing about it was the rigging of a 'chais decompression sling', complete with arm and foot loops, from Fiona's scientific line.

Rob Palmer: So was that it? Bish and I swam up the North Passage after a team had swum the bottom photographing, and finding nothing, we spiralled down a boulder ruckle near the far end, reaching 220 ft (66 m), and seeing a continuation to at least 250 ft (75 m). It seemed that everyone, whether breathing heliox or air, came out with different ideas of what was 'final', and what 'went'. Perhaps the sheer drama of the cave created its own narcotic effect, and vision was channelled into what the diver wanted to see, or thought he saw, whatever he was breathing. There was no doubt that breathing heliox at depth created a level-headedness and awareness that was lacking on air, but there were still high levels of anxiety and a sense of urgency on each excursion into the further reaches of Stargate that negated the opportunity for a calm appraisal of the cave.

In mid-August, after we had finished the exploration of El Dorado, and Bill and the Carmellan team had both left the island, Richard and I swam south in Stargate for one last attempt at the end. Gathering the usual crowd of local urchins on the surface, we lugged our eight tanks across the now well-worn trail to the entrance, and kitted up in the afternoon sun. The entrance seemed silent after the bustle of the filming and science dives. The generators and computers were gone, the large oxygen tanks carried back to base, with only the cut shrubbery to indicate that something had happened here. A few months, and even this would be regrown. The thermometer read 102° F (39° C) on the surface, and we kitted up slowly, half-in, half-out of the water. We each carried a single Acurex stage cylinder of heliox, and two air-filled 80s, and had each placed a separate oxygen cylinder on the shotline at the entrance.

The staging point in Stargate's South Passage. Air stage cylinders were left here before dives were made down the narrow gap into the deeper cave beyond. *(Photo: Rob Palmer)*

We coasted along the south line, taking a few photographs as far as the constriction. There we dumped both the camera and my air stage tank. Richard continued to wear his, having started with the other tank slightly under-pressure due to a leaking valve on the surface. Swimming into the big chamber beyond, we came to the point where my deep line diverged from the American line laid by Mark Madden and Roger Werner the year before. Faced with the choice of descending into relatively known territory, or continuing to the end of the American line, we chose to do the latter, aware that they had still regarded the end of the cave as 'open'.

This was a mistake. Instead of ending at the next boulder pile, as we had thought, it disappeared down a crevice at the west side. So we followed this, slightly against my better judgement, but remembering the potential for continuing and deepening cave beyond. We soon ran into a maze of breakdown. Ducking under a huge poised slab, quite impressed with their nerve if nothing else, we reached their final tie-off after about 100 ft (30 m). We looked at each other, and what passed for the 'way on', and both switched to heliox.

The way on was not, in fact, very obvious at all, but by descending carefully to the right and swinging our new line cautiously across a huge slab, I managed to zig-zag slowly and gingerly down through a constriction to a short vertical crack between the breakdown and the west wall raising sediment from the slabs as I did so. This narrow 2 ft (0.6 m)-wide slot between boulders and wall led down to 220 ft (66 m). At the base of the crack, the only way on was back into the 'hanging death' of the breakdown, squeezing between blocks covered with a thick layer of black silt in a cave which had long ago lost its attraction. Finally, almost back at the east wall, the boulders closed down, and the only way on I could see lay through a tiny gap about 15 in (38 cm) wide. Beyond that the route enlarged slightly, and the waters were still clear, but the position I was in was fast getting beyond the bounds of sanity. I turned, to signal to Richard that this was it, and saw only a dark and blinding silt cloud. As this rolled in around me, all visibility instantly went. I was wedged 225 ft (67.5 m) down in a tiny boulder chamber, unable to see the way back out.

I hoped to God that Richard had had the sense to back out when he saw how conditions were developing. If he had let go the line, he would be in real trouble. As indeed I might be . . . if the line had slipped between the boulders along the circuitous route between me and the start of the choke, I'd be in *very* serious trouble. I groped my way blindly through the rock maze, reeling in the thin line that my entire trust was placed in, and using my arms and shoulders to feel the shape of the passage in front, trying to avoid any place that might ensnare equipment. My gear scrunched between rock surfaces as I forced myself gingerly through the final constriction and back across the slab to the American tie-off point.

From there the route was easier. Rather shaken, I emerged from the clouds of the choke back into the big chamber. Richard's lights shone about 60 ft (18 m) above me. I swam round at about 200 ft (60 m), slowly unwinding myself, and looking for alternative ways on. The only ones were deep, down toward the bottom of the chamber, and I cursed myself for being lured down the American line. I rose to follow Richard, to collect my stage tank beyond the first constriction, and swim back down the shallower passages to the entrance. The waters had a green translucence, legacy of a dye test Pete Smart had carried out a couple of days before.

We paid our dues, and finally rose to the oxygen stops with only a few pounds of pressure left in the heliox tanks. As we finally surfaced, about 1½ hours later, one of the oxygen tanks slipped from our overloaded grasp and sank slowly into the depths, leaving only a trail of tiny bubbles from a slightly-leaking valve trickling through our outstretched fingers. We gazed at the silver stream of oxygen, continuing to mark the wake of the tank's descent long after it hit bottom, joining a small and growing pile of lost equipment, including Yanto's sunglasses (a vocal point of order each time anyone entered the water), and sighed.

Funnily enough, the tiny wake of bubbles saved us a recovery attempt. As the tiny leak slowly emptied the tank, it became more and more buoyant. Visiting the cave the following day, there was the cylinder, floating bottom up on the top of the lake, still with pressure in it!

So Stargate's final reaches had eluded us. We'd managed 320 ft (96 m) with the rebreathers beneath the entrance, and a little over 250 ft (75 m) elsewhere. By that depth, there was little stalagmite anyway – some sort of event in the history of the cave seems to have made the 200–225 ft (60–67.5 m) area a general cut-off point for stalagmite and stalactite growth. Perhaps sea-levels were only below that for a very short time, or perhaps there is some other explanation? Some day, someone may find the elusive way through the boulders and will be able to tell.

One interesting thing we did discover on all our deep dives was the need for a 'plus-one metre decompression stop'. Long, deep mixed-gas dives with oxygen decompression take it out of the system, and definitely require a good hour's snooze afterwards to allow the body to rest as the last of those final tiny bubbles were exhausted from the blood. While the rest of the crew got on with pumping tanks and making dinner, we rapidly became experts at 'hammock decompression'.

On 28th July 1987 Chris Howes and Judith Calford had rolled in, bleary-eyed from their trip across on the mailboat. We gave them a taste of what was to come by packing them immediately off to Stargate while Bill and I got ready for the final attempt at El Dorado the following day. Brad would be supporting us down to 200 ft (60 m), and the whole afternoon was spent lugging the fourteen tanks needed for the dive through the jungle to the lake.

The 29th was a pivotal day. The Carmellan team were flying out, and the emphasis was switching back to open-circuit diving. In a few days, Pete Smart and the geology team were departing for North Andros, and the biologists were beginning to arrive. After the obligatory team photograph, farewells were made and the truck sent rolling towards El Dorado. The final bags of gear were carried in by the diving team, with Chris, Judith and Pat acting as porters.

Bill was using his steel 'double hundreds', 2,200 psi tanks jacked up to 3,000 psi, and filled with heliox. One air-filled Luxfer 80 completed his breathing supply. I intended wearing two back-mounted Acurex containing air, and two side-mounted Acurex with heliox in them. Brad, who was coming down to 200 ft (60 m) to help take pictures and who would be responsible for setting in the four oxygen decompression tanks, wore three of the 80s, each containing air.

We struggled into most of this in the water, using a large inflatable yellow li-lo as 'advance base'. It took 45 minutes to get everything on and working smoothly. Bill took his camera, with Brad holding a custom-built 400-watt strobe on the end of a long lead, and they followed me into the cave.

The drop-down through the mirk was fast, and we met again in the clear canyon beneath. I led into the deeper section, with the strobe flashing behind me like sheet lightning, starkly illuminating the cave for fractional moments of intense clarity. The cave seemed a little different, perhaps because we were focusing more on the roof than the floor this time. The plan was to stay as high as possible for as long as possible, then go down, but the roof denied us this luxury, dropping inexorably. I tied the new reel on to our old line at about 160 ft (48 m). The line promptly jammed around the reel, and I cut it and retied the ends. Still jammed. I took my knife out, and levered the spool-axle free, to unhitch the tangled cord. Success – the reel flows freely again. Breaking open two cylumes, glowing chemical lights in waterproof tubes, I looped these on the line and swam across the chamber to the west wall. While Bill passed the camera equipment to Brad, I fastened the line to a flake on the wall. Another tangle; a faulty reel. I suddenly felt I wanted to try to sort this out before I changed to heliox, out of curiosity to see whether narcosis was affecting my co-ordination much. It took a minute or two to clear the reel, for which we undoubtedly paid a time penalty later (as Bill, who had already changed over, pointedly remarked afterwards). Brad floated in the water, watching, as Bill and I began the long descent, both now breathing from the heliox tanks.

With the new perspective of knowing where the roof was, I could now see that the chamber was in fact still one huge canyon, with the roof dropping, almost to meet the floor at somewhere over 250 ft (75 m) ahead. At a little below 270 ft (80 m), we traversed the vast chaotic floor. We passed the gap I descended previously, and moved over above the boulder pile beyond. Rocks lay everywhere, and it seemed as though the walls were gradually closing in. The cave became smaller and more solid. By −290 ft (−87 m), there were only two possible ways on, a narrow rift along the west wall, and a hole between breakdown slabs in front. I thrust my head into the rift. Solid wall in front. Edging back, raising fine silt from the rocks, I moved to try the Hole. Bill hung back, a few feet higher, keeping my exit clear.

The Hole looked as though it might choke too, and pushing further into it this deep would be too chancy. I tried to tie the line off at the side of the Hole, but could find nothing to fix it to. A small boulder was not security enough, and the water clouds fast with silt. Back off! Bill was above me in clear water. Between us was a good, solid outcrop, and the line went round that several times before I cut it and tied a knot. Bill began his survey out, following the line, but I took a last look round for ways on. There was another smaller hole that might go, beneath a block, but not with back-mounts. It would be desperate, and might also dead-end. Beside this was the boulder ridge leading over to the passage I went down last time. Unless there is something much higher up, the cave ends here.

Thirty-three minutes into the dive, I started my slow ascent, the rate checked by the flickering red light on the Decobrain, which flashed at me if I rose faster than the safe rate. The green glow of the cyalumes is a star in the firmament, high up, and far away. I followed the floor up, looking for the bones, but somehow missed them. I realized for the first time just how slow an ascent from this depth must be – it takes much more time, and much more breathing gas, than the descent – and I realized too that it's worth leaving a greater reserve of gas for the swim up and out than just a third. At 150 ft (45 m) I could see Bill's silhouette well above me, survey over. I felt strangely flat, disappointed that the cave had not led us that little way further, below 300 ft (90 m), forgetting that it still ranked as one of the world's classics, and one of the deepest and remotest cave-diving explorations yet made.

The decompression seems eternal, 3½ hours of dues for a little over 30 minutes of diving. The Decobrain abandoned me several minutes before I regained the shotline, protesting at the depth and length of the dive. I bet myself that not many had experienced that happening, but I had strayed well outside its territory. We were now on US Navy Exceptional Exposure tables, and calculating our own stops underwater. The oxygen tanks drew closer as we rose, and we switched to them at 30 ft (9 m). At 10 ft (3 m), the underwater earphone comes down, and I have 40 minutes of the Oyster Band before someone forgets to turn the tape over. Silence falls again. Bish and Yanto appear, the 'Dangerous Brothers', buddy-breathing on a single octopus set, and wave at us. They took it in turns to descend the shotline to look at the canyon 60 ft (18 m) down. I take a few pictures of Bill. He takes some of me. We wait some more.

Finally, at 3.45, we broke surface and swam wearily back across to the ladder. It took some time to dekit and haul up, then more to carry out. Big loads after a long dive are not to be recommended, heavy activity can bring on decompression sickness even after a dive is over, but we split them down and did each run twice. Brad, who after surfacing three hours before had gone to Stargate to help with the filming, returned and helped us too, great guy that he is. At length we were finished, practically as well as physically, and drove back through the early dusk to dinner and cold beers and that plus-one-metre decompression stop, in swaying hammocks by the sea.

A few days later, out of curiosity, I took a couple of 80s through the constriction in Jellyfish Lake to see if it might be possible to push a connection with El Dorado from there. The way in was pretty committing, and only *just* possible with the two side mounts. Beyond, a series of fresh-looking rifts and boulder piles led on several levels to impassable chokes, none deeper than 120 ft (36 m). With plenty of air, and good lights, I looked in every possible place, but found no way on. Any route through to El Dorado lay beneath the massive boulder pile at the start of the cave; all these high-level rifts were far too recent. I saw the Chickcharnie bone pile, and collected some of the fragile bones for proper analysis.

Out of curiosity, after squeezing out again, I rose into the upper levels I'd looked in briefly the year before. Poking inquisitively in each cranny, I found a second 'owl-nest', a mound of bones beneath a ledge at a depth of about 20 ft (6 m). The nest itself had long rotted, but the pile of *hutia* bones cast from it, that represented countless owl dinners, had remained. The ledge above overhung, the bones could not have fallen from above, and must have lain beneath the actual nest itself. Twenty feet (6 m) below current sea-levels means that the now extinct giant owls used the nest site somewhere over 10,000 years ago, a long time for left-overs to hang around.

I pushed 65–100 ft (20–30 m) into the upper section, past several large brown *Lucifuga,* the biggest blind cave fish I had seen yet. The cave got increasingly shallower until, just before it became too narrow, I emerged in a small, enclosed airspace. Fine, thread-like roots emerged from cracks in the light-brown roof, and the air, though stale, was breathable. It was the only completely enclosed air-filled cavity we found – an isolated pocket sealed off from the world outside shortly after the giant owls had been driven from their nest by the rising post-glacial seas, while mankind was beginning its long haul towards civilization and coming to terms with the Flood that forced him, like the *hutia* and the Chickcharnies, from his ancient hunting grounds in lands newly drowned by the sea.

CHAPTER ELEVEN

Sanctuary

S ANCTUARY IS a lonely place. It lies some distance from the road, and there is no easy track through the forest. What path there is zig-zags haphazardly across the ankle-breaking landscape, bestrewn with sharp vines to snag legs, and poisonwood to brush unwary skin. The dark entrance pool is close-mouthed, overhung by limestone cliffs and obscured by a brown tangle of Bahamian scrub, by air plants and orchids, a silent gate to an aquatic underworld of unusual and awesome splendour. Drab, brown gobies lurk torpidly in crevices, land crabs haul buff-coloured carapaces across lichenous walls, and a thousand mosquitoes hum in dreamy anticipation of something warm-blooded to suck.

Pessimistically, we hauled a single tank through this thick, razor-floored jungle between the east coast and the cave mouth. The tank had a 'Y-valve', a twin takeoff which allowed two separate demand valves to be fitted, a back-up breathing system being essential under countless tons of solid rock. While I checked four lights and all the other paraphernalia, Pete Glanvill tied the end of the line to what looked like the most solid and immovable of several flakes of rock. I wriggled into harness in a twilight cleft, a more confining situation than any so far, half on land and half in water, and floated in the sombre pool for a moment, recovering my breath. A new cave always makes me more apprehensive – it is always a little more irrationally daunting. I garbled goodbye though a mouthful of mouthpiece, and committed myself to the cold and enveloping gloom.

These first few moments of a cave dive are always the worst. The anticipation of equipment failure, the racing pulse and heightened, nervous breathing, the gradual adjustment of eyes to the darkness . . . Only as mind, body and equipment slide into tune does the environment begin to register, and the dark recedes far enough for the conscious mind to regain some control. It's worth taking a few moments to float below the surface, get adjusted, to speed the process along. Being methodical helps – a kind of self-hypnosis, I suppose.

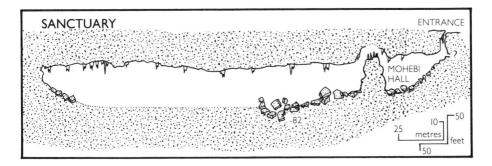

The mists dispersed into a now-familiar blur in the water, where freshwater and saltwater mingle. Stones appeared below, rough limestone slabs overlain by a dusky powder of organic silt, harsh white shapes etched gently by centuries of fragile decay. The boulder scree disappeared steeply into the unyielding shade, but across the small chamber a narrow canyon lured me on. Comparatively shallow, with the gauge only reading 80 ft (24 m), it was obviously the way to go.

Moving weightlessly through the void, I picked the western wall and followed it, heading south. On my right, ancient runs of flowstone stood out in sharp relief, fretted by centuries of resolution. The line was tied to a small flake of this rock, delicately, as I waited for it to shatter. It held. More cord rattled from the reel.

Ahead, a solid wall appeared, soaring up from the unseen floor. My heart sank – so soon? I'd felt in my bones that the cave would go further.

But no, it was no wall at all, but an island, a peak, a ludicrous underwater mountain, inside a chamber, deep inside a cave. My head shook in conscious wonderment. Astonishing! On both sides, the void fell into darkness, framed by the vaulted arch of the cavern walls. In the centre of this underground hall, a mountain rose to a small plateau, where stalagmites stook like crystal sarsens, stone pillars reaching into the dim clouds of the sulphurous mixing zone.

I flew round the island on its west side, floating over the unfathomed depths. The pillar closest me was fluted and castled, a giant candle of dripping wax, cast into crystal flowstone. Stirred by the rising exhaust bubbles, a rain of fine debris began to fall in from above, like silent, drifting snow. In front, the chamber walls closed in, and the cave reverted to passageway, a high canyon. I finned for a few yards more, to a stalactite boss jutting out of the east wall, and decided I was far enough out for one tank. Time to go home. The line was tied and cut and I turned back, surveying as I went. A solitary blind cave-fish watched me as I swam again across the huge wall. White fins rippled along its spine in silent waves, a tiny leviathan in the sombre firmament.

Back beneath the entrance, I looked for and found a way on to the north, through a small gap across from the descending shotline. Then, glancing casually round the rocks that floored the cave, I saw four or five long bones. Thigh bones, I thought, and saw a rib beyond. Poking around a little further, a large animal skull appeared – either horse or cow – and the bones seemed a little more in context. A smaller skull, maybe goat, lay nearby, and several other small bones poked out of the rock. Then round the corner, wedged between two boulders, lay a human skull. I decided not to mess around any further. With a last glance, I surfaced slowly, looking for walls and seeing none.

'Oh, wow,' was all I could say, in a muted voice, as I broke surface. Lyrical description was always one of my strong points.

'Was that "Ugh . . . waurgh", or "*OH WOW*"?' asked Judith. I grinned at her. As we thrashed our way back through the scrub, she asked if I had thought of a name for the cave.

'Sanctuary,' I said.

Stargate had given us a lot. Like a woman who allows her body to be used for the education and joy of her lovers and the growth and nourishment of her children, we had used her too well. Undoubtedly we had learnt much, but we had left her no longer virginal. The scars of our work showed only too clearly in places. Sanctuary was the nearest thing we had to Stargate. I wondered whether we could leave her unmarred?

Two days later, after a long survey dive in Elvenhome, we were back at Sanctuary. The day was one of the hottest yet, with temperatures in the upper 90s° F (35–8° C). The walk in was disgustingly sweaty, the struggle into gear more so. I was planning a long dive, and anticipating a long decompression. Gallons of perspiration ran from me just climbing into my drysuit, partially replaced by long pulls at the waterflask. With thermal underwear beneath, I felt like a portable sauna. Pete Glanvill was coming with me, to help photograph as far as the chamber, which we had decided to call 'Mohebi Hall' in recognition of the great generosity of our major sponsor, Zainal Mohebi. In his bright yellow-and-red wetsuit, Pete was only slightly less close to terminal heatstroke than I. At last, sweat blinding me, I could take it no longer, and fell arse-first into the water, floating face up with arms and legs fully extended, swiping mosquitoes in desultory fashion until the heat drained away. Starting a long dive in such a state is not to be recommended – the dilated blood vessels in an overheated body can increase the rate at which nitrogen is absorbed, and so increase considerably the possibility of getting bent. Pete, our doctor, took continuous pleasure in reminding me of this.

While Pete made a final gear check, I tied an oxygen tank 20 ft (6 m) down on the shotline for use on decompression, then set off into the entrance chamber to photograph the bones, breathing air from a third stage tank to save my two main tanks for the exploration ahead. Pete joined me moments later, and quickly turned up another scattered collection of human bones. I took two quick shots of these, then pointed down the passage. In Mohebi Hall, I took several pictures of Pete drifting surrealistically in among the pillars on the peak. As silt clouds drifted in from above, Pete indicated that he had better be going out.

His lights disappeared, leaving me alone in the Hall as I unclipped the stage tank and placed it carefully down amongst the stalagmites on the rise. Moving out of the chamber, down the continuing passage at about −130 ft (−40 m), I came to the stalactite outcrop at the end of the line. Tying on a new reel, I swam below the stalactite and into a wide and vast canyon, heading south.

Abruptly the thin exploration line jammed, caught around the reel and my survey slate. To free myself quickly, I cut it, unravelled the knot, and retied the ends. A few feet later it happened again. As I repeated the exercise, the handpiece of my main light struck the wall sharply. The bulb blew.

By now, having used quite a bit of air in sorting out the line, I was feeling pretty pissed off. I began wondering whether cave or gods were conspiring against me. One helmet torch was expiring, the other was freshly charged, and bright. I had an extra one on my harness. That meant I could dive on one of the smaller torches only, and keep one as a spare. That was half as many as I should have for a solo exploration. In a mixture of anger and despair I knew each dive had to count. By the beam of one small torch, I swam on into the cave.

I expected the cave to choke with every stroke of my fins, but it kept on going. The roof steadily dropped, and I found myself swimming at 130 ft (40 m) almost without realizing. I rose a little, to try and save on decompression, though the few feet gained seemed a little ridiculous. The stalactite formations were impressive, and I used my camera to photograph a couple of the more exotic ones. The pale beam of the one small torch made the cave more oppressive, and shadows flickering across the rough rock made the walls look threateningly loose. At length, pushing 'thirds' somewhat in the hope of emptying the reel, I came to the rational decision that I should have reached much earlier. I hadn't enough light or air to be where I was. I stopped at the next convenient stalagmite belay to tie off the line. Ahead, the cave soared on, high above, deep below, dark as midnight in front.

Anxious but elated, I began to head back, making a perfunctory survey as I went. Much of the canyon was narrow, only 9–12 ft (3–4 m) wide, but equally much was twice that width, a huge chasm that disappeared into the darkness of the 'danger zone' below 200 ft (60 m). A good place to bring heliox!

The knots in the new line appeared, then the belay, after 53 tags – over 520 ft (156 m) of new cave. I felt a brief moment of regret at not finishing the reel, though my tanks now both read below their reserve mark. But, shortly beyond, a metal obelisk amongst the crystal on the peak of Mohebi Hall, my stage tank crept into view. Suddenly I had more than enough air to get out on, to decompress with, even without the oxygen tank at the entrance. Had my big light been working, I would undoubtedly have gone for it, and laid out the few remaining metres of line on the reel.

I picked up a thighbone from the second pile of human remains, for dating and analysis, and ascended the shotline. Changing to the oxygen tank at −20 ft (−6 m), I settled down for another 72 minutes of hanging in the water beneath the entrance, almost as long as the dive itself. The adrenalin drained away slowly, along with body heat. I began to shiver. As I rose to the final stop, the small underwater speaker we had connected to a Walkman floated down to meet me. The Hebridean rhythms of Runrig came down the wire as I hung at 10 ft (3 m) with 'Recovery' – a beautiful song about contemplating the dawn mists over the island of Skye. Two and a half hours after entering the water, I moved the last few metres to the surface, and the bugs.

We didn't get back to Sanctuary for a while. Problems with airfreighting the rebreathers out kept me on the phone to Nassau much of the next day, and we then had to spend time out at sea, working with the marine team. On 14 August we were joined by the British High Commissioner to Nassau, Colin Mays, and his son, Nick. Colin had taken pains to convince us that his visit was more in the way of a holiday, a short break from Nassau routine, and he wanted very much to be treated as part of the team.

On the excuse that the marine Holes were probably more interesting for a first stop, we launched both Zodiacs, and took Colin and Nick out to snorkel two of our favourite ocean Holes, Shark Hole and Bidet Hole. Shark Hole is a dramatic vertical pit, named after the 10 ft (3 m) lemon shark that takes occasional residence on a ledge 60 ft (18 m) down. The pit itself continues to 200 ft (60 m), where unexplored and very narrow passages lead off. The currents here are fierce, whirlpooling in, strong enough at full flow to send the exhaust bubbles from a diver's regulator hurtling down into the cave instead of up to the surface of the sea. The surrounding reef is set in water rather deeper than most of the lagoon caves, and the diversity and sheer number of fish reflects this. The entrance is a photographer's paradise.

Bidet Hole takes its name from a rather unfortunate coral formation near the entrance, the shape of which had triggered an immediate chord in Mary Stafford Smith's sense of humour on the 1986 reconnaissance. Then, I'd looked a little way insde the entrance, exploring a roomy chamber on a single tank without seeing any definite way on. The currents were good, however, and while the others snorkelled round and teased the fish, I thought I would take the opportunity to explore properly.

The cave was inflowing quite firmly, though not so strongly that I felt I couldn't handle a swim out against the flow. The entrance, cool and enticing, lay through a twin arch of tumbled elkhorn coral, past a huge school of silver jacks, down into a wide cavern. There, the tunnel curved to the right, sloping slowly down beneath a roof covered with pastel sponges and the sharp single polyps of *Phyllangia* coral. Scarlet shrimps scurried across the rough walls, dappled cowries grazed among hydroids and bryzoans, and sleepy noctural blue-striped grunts lurked in crevices in the twilight zone, waiting for night to fall outside. But after the first hundred free or so, the sloping rift turned to a vertical crack, and the way on lay through a narrow slot at a depth of 40 ft (12 m). The current went down this and, like the White Rabbit in *Alice Through the Looking Glass,* I fed myself into it feet first, trying not to do too much damage to the multi-coloured sponges encrusting the walls of the crevice, or to myself.

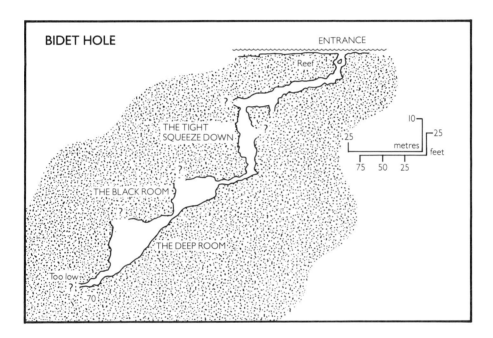

A slight ledge at 70 ft (21 m) gave me a pause for a brief re-adjustment of gear, but then the squeeze continued, even more claustrophobically than before. My back and my front both scraped the rock as I slid down through an even narrower section, and I began to wonder about getting out. The hoses on my demand valves snagged repeatedly on small flakes of rock, invisible in the silt cloud, and my tanks clanged repeatedly on the walls, ringing echoes through the water.

Palmer sandwich, I thought uneasily.

At −100 ft (−30 m) I hit 'floor', a steeply descending tube, a slight widening of the rift over a sand-covered boulder floor. Getting both bearings and breath, I felt better, and went on. At −150 ft (−45 m), the passage came out high up on the wall of a large chamber. But good old Murphy had been putting the line on the reel that day . . . making sure it ran out just as I emerged into the big cavern, hanging in the roof by one wall, with no other side in sight. I floated in ebony, feeling not a little cheated. This sort of thing happens just a bit too often to be coincidence. Gods exist, and I think they have a perverse sense of humour.

I reeled the line back in until I found a belay, near the base of the constricted rift. The inflowing current meant that, paradoxically, I could see more going out than coming in – the silt stirred by my entry was now being washed further into the cave. Getting up was just as awkward as coming down, but at least I could now see where to aim for. I emerged at the top of the rift with scratched tanks and a couple of rips in my wetsuit, but otherwise intact.

Decompression was spent with a macro lens, taking shots of corals, shrimps and sponges before joining the two others to scoot back onshore for lunch. One of the pleasant, and slightly peculiar, rewards of Bahamian cave exploration is that despite the utter isolation of the deep underwater caverns, working at the limits of technology and endeavour, one need never be too far from a cold beer. After all, there has to be some reward for coping with all the deific humour!

The following day found us back in Sanctuary. Colin and Nick learned about Andros bush the hard way, struggling through it beneath a midday sun with my diving tanks and weightbelt on their backs. Full team members by now, no special treatment at all.

Colin Mays, the British High Commissioner, helps Rob Palmer into the water at Sanctuary Blue Hole. *(Photo: Chris Howes FRPS)*

This dive was essentially for science. We wanted to see both how deep the cave went, and whether or not there were any deep stalagmites. I had two tanks of heliox, one of air, and intended to use the oxygen tank already down the cave to decompress on. Clad in a black, heat-absorbing drysuit, I was once again glad to get underwater.

I drifted to the base of the pit, and took a few photographs of the bones. Then, leaving the camera on the shotline, I headed down the cave. Swimming slowly round Mohebi Hall, I could see with the brighter light that the floor on the west side trailed down to nearly 200 ft (60 m), and that the stalagmite pillars went a long way down the slope.

As I swam across the Hall, I came close to swimming into a small writhing creature, just like a swimming centipede, in mid-water. A *Remipede*, one of a group of small cave dwellers whose discovery in 1980 signalled the creation of a whole new order of crustacea. This encounter was quite exciting – only one of the little white creatures had been seen on Andros so far, in Stargate, and this was definitely a different type, possibly one of a species called *Godzillius*, because of its much larger size – 1.5 in (4 cm) a giant among its fellows. Who says biologists don't have a sense of humour?

I left the small creature to its lonely dance and swam on. At the end of the first line, below the stalactite outcrop, the cave walls fell away from each other into an apparently fathomless void. Stalactites hung from the walls here, their tips pointing into the depths. Thousands of years ago, droplets of water fell from their tips through space, spattering down to the unseen floor, depositing a calcite covering on whatever surface they hit. But just how deep such stalagmites could form was still a mystery. Perhaps the tiny droplets simply splashed unseen into the still waters of the Ice Age caves?

I tied a new line reel on to the wall, and purged air from my drysuit, deliberately losing buoyancy. Slowly, line winding from the reel, I sank into the darkness. Narcosis insinuated itself into my consciousness as the needle on the depth gauge moved round its dial. By the torch-light, I could see the shapes of giant boulders jammed across the passage below, blocks the size of caravans in a chaos of shadowy disorder. At 140 ft (42 m), the walls changed colour from white to the darker, duller brown of depth, and the atmosphere altered, grew more grim, more claustrophobic. Silt rose from the walls as I stirred the calm of the water, grey clouds that found my wake and followed me down.

Just below 200 ft (60 m) I changed to heliox, carefully checking the colour-coding of the yellow demand valve I placed in my mouth. The mists of narcosis fell away in the now customary three breaths, and the rocks around me grew three-dimensional, suddenly even more jagged and disordered as my brain cleared.

Two hundred and seventy feet (80 m) below the island, the sides were sheer and smooth and dark. They went on down, into the night, held apart by huge blocks that had once been walls. These boulders were now jammed too closely together to squeeze through, though one gap held a promise of 300 ft (90 m). Even as I contemplated the commitment, a cloud of fine silt crept insidiously in to hide the narrow opening. I could barely see the reel. There were no stalagmites here, the last ones had faded out just below 200 ft (60 m). This alien place held nothing for me. It felt oppressive, almost malevolent. Up seemed the best direction. I ran away.

The ascent was interminable. Winding in the line and watching the extra minutes clock up on the dive counter took all my attention. A small red light blinked at me whenever I moved too fast, telling me that bubbles might be forming in my blood. I felt that I had fallen into a dream – one of those half-nightmares where you move, but make no progress. There was little to tell me I was rising, the cave was hidden behind silt clouds, and my bubbles raced ahead, leaving me behind. The reel kept turning, turning, winding in line . . .

At length the cave cleared, the swim became horizontal, the walls were white again, and time restarted. Mohebi Hall, and its tannic halocline clouds came and went, fine bacterial debris from above already beginning to drape the pillars in a dark coat of algal snow. In the bone room, my first stops were deep, and I found three more skulls before rising to meet the oxygen tank. Decompression took longer than the dive itself. After two hours of swimming and hanging out on the shotline, rising the last 10 ft (3 m) to sunshine and sound was deliverance itself.

We knew now how deep the cave was, and the next thing to do was to explore beyond the 'end'. Three days later, at 5.15 in the evening, Pete Glanvill and I sank into the gloomy entrance pool again. Pete would once more be accompanying me as far as Mohebi Hall, after which I intended to head off alone down the South Passage and see where it led to. The nearest Blue Hole to the south was several thousand feet beyond the end of the line, and the dive could be quite a long one. Because of this, I wore four tanks, two of the high pressure Acurex tanks on my back and two aluminium 80s on my sides. Fast swimming would be out of the question today.

So, kick away the crab that's nibbling on the line. Submerge. Swim . . .

. . . I handed Pete the cameras and waved goodbye. Mohebi Hall disappeared behind me as I swam slowly up the cave, past the line junction, and into the main South Passage.

Cruising up the canyon, hands clasped in front of me, was one of the most delicious experiences of the expedition. Everything was securely in place, and I felt more than usual that surreal impression of flight. The walls soared down into perpetual night, and arched over a few metres above my head to collide in pristine cascades of crystal flowstone. In the light of the big torch beam, I could see all that I had missed on the previous exploration, and the view was sumptuous and immense. Straw-thin columns linked stalagmites and stalactites on the walls, cascading waves of flowstone overhung the void, great slabs of wall rock hung at potentially disastrous angles, fragile colossi waiting to tumble at the merest nudge –

until one saw the stalactites growing on them, and realized that this gargantuan avalanche had been waiting to occur for thousands of years.

How do you describe the thrill of being utterly alone? Outside, in the other world, there was so much to do, politics to play, egos to soothe, problems to solve. Now, here there was only me, and this timeless, eternal cave. I felt part of things, a tolerated guest. Benjamin had been driven by the thrill of discovering new places, the search for underwater formations, the curiosity of what lay round the next bend. There was that in me too, I guess, but the main reason I did this was for the inutterable joy of being truly, absolutely alive, in a way that no social or artificial stimulus can ever offer. This feeling comes sometimes on high, lonely mountains, deep out in the ocean seas, in dawn sunlight filtering through cool spring woodlands, in such places when alone and utterly at peace with nature. It comes doubly so when commitment is total. I belonged here. Tenseness slipped away, I entered a state of near total relaxation. Blissfully, I cruised the waters of Lethe.

The line led on for an indeterminable distance. I couldn't remember a tenth of this cave – even the fact that the line followed the East Wall was new to me, so little had I seen by the glow of one small torch last time. At one point I began to wonder whether narcosis had caught me, or whether someone had snuck in and laid more line. I knew this was ridiculous, but I found it difficult to accept that I could have forgotten – and missed – so much. At length the line swung over to the West Wall, and the small familiar stalagmites of the tie-off appeared. By now the roof had dropped steeply, and I floated at 130 ft (40 m). I tied on a new reel, switched to a fresh air tank, and moved on.

And the cave stopped. Suddenly, and less than 30 ft (9 m) from my tie-off. The relaxation vanished – I felt sick, and partly relieved. The utter clarity of the water had made me unusually conscious of every metre on the swim in, and despite the calm, I'd been unable to switch off my awareness of distance, as I might have done in murkier water. Now things had begun to happen again, I felt a long way from day, and loneliness bore a sharper countenance. Below me, at about 180 ft (54 m), rocks sloped back down the passage, fading out of sight to invisible depths beneath my line. No obvious – or easy – way on there. Above, the roof rose, and I rose with it, looping the line around a flake to guide me back down through the silt that stirred as my bubbles hit the roof. At −125 ft (−37.5 m), a thin and very constricted crack offered a chance, but not with the amount of gear I wore. Above, the cave was even more constricted, and too committing. This looked like the end.

I cut and tied the line, then dropped back down to the belay. I decided to swim as high in the passage as I could during the journey out, to cut down as much as possible on decompression time. About 30–40 ft (9–12 m) back down the passage the roof suddenly rose and, peering back, there was a suggestion of a way on here, a small opening that might lead over the top of the choke, but within the mixing zone. There was nothing obviously visible in the shallower brown-stained waters, and I decided not to attempt to press on further.

Swimming about 30 ft (9 m) above the line, I was astounded by the profusion of formations in the roof of the cave – more stunning than any of the other Andros caves. At one point, mouth-watering crystal curtains cascaded in waves down the walls, at another a slender, 10 ft (3 m) long, 3 in (7.6 cm) thick stalactite hung vertically down the centre of the passage, an inverted Excalibur anchored in the stone. This went on, galleries of white, a jewelled cave, until constriction grew and I was forced down to the line again, just before Mohebi Hall.

Decompression lasted until twilight; it was almost dark as I broke surface. The mosquitoes – and the words of comment from the waiting and increasingly anaemic support team – were appalling, and my wetsuit stayed on for the hurried stumble across the darkened landscape and until we were safely home. I was exhausted. I could do little for some time but drink cold beer until I found the strength to strip the suit off and resume position with the glass.

We had a dilemma. We had to do something about the bones, but we weren't sure what. If they were the remains of dark ritual, or grimmer relics of more recent murder, we might have problems with the locals on our hands. Some things are most diplomatically forgotten about, or subtly ignored. But if they were older, the relics of Pre-Columbian civilization in the Bahamas, then the find was of considerable archaeological significance.

It was almost impossible to tell much about their age from the apparent condition of the bones – other than that they were not that fresh. Tannic staining, once flesh and outer coverings (presuming there had been any) had gone, would have taken place fairly quickly, though one or two of the animal skulls were still white, suggesting that Sanctuary was still occasionally used to dispose of unwanted carcasses. What made it more confusing was the presence of several large stones, with lengths of rope rising from them, with small and rather suspicious-looking loops tied in the ends. Were these just used to weigh the more recent of the animal carcasses down, or had they been ankle-loops, tied to people? At least one of the ropes was of nylon – not a fabric in evidence five hundred years ago, when Arawak Indians inhabited the islands.

Arawaks did not usually bury their dead underwater, either. Their creation legend told of their entrapment in a cave, from which they were freed from the clutches of a guarding giant by the sun and moon, themselves escapees from a second cave. So Arawak dead had been buried in dry caves, where their families could visit them and lay offerings down. This could present a certain difficulty in 70 ft (20 m) of water. However, two other 'underwater' burials had been found, one on Grand Bahama, where several Arawak skeletons were discovered in an air-filled lake chamber, one of the entrances to the Lucayan Caverns, one of the world's most extensive networks of underwater cave passages. These remains had been plundered by ghoulish souvenir hunters before the site could be excavated, and so any understanding of who they were or why they were there had been lost. A second site, in the Turks and Caicos Islands, had been discovered, but still awaited excavation.

But there might be other reasons for an Arawak burial here. There were few dry caves on South Andros, and this might be the next best option. Or perhaps the bones were from criminals, ritually strangled and given perfunctory burial? Or victims of plague?

Or suicides? When Columbus and his Spaniards discovered the Bahamas – the islands in the great *baja mar*, the 'shallow seas' – they found a well–established society that had existed there in relative peace and prosperity for hundreds of years, a culture with a tradition of ocean sailing in huge canoes, with pastoral and fishing skills that told of a long involvement with islands and seas. Their stories told of a race of white-skinned gods who would come from the east in ships with wings (sails). They greeted their gods with gifts and delight.

The calculated annihilation of the Bahamian Arawaks is one of the most disgusting stories of European empire. Shipped in hundreds to the silver mines of Cuba and Hispaniola by the *conquistadores,* they died in droves. Within a generation, the Spanish explorer Ponce de Leon, sailing in the northern Bahamas on his search for the legendary Fountain of Youth, reported that the islands were bare. Only one old woman, on a small isolated cay, could be found. Wonderful thing, Christian civilization.

Many Arawaks, the very base of their culture – their gods – having so callously and despicably proved false, committed suicide in utter despair. Could Sanctuary be the resting place of some such forsaken unfortunates?

I called Neil Sealey, a lecturer at the College of the Bahamas in Nassau and an active member of the Bahamian Historical Society. Neil told me that if the remains were Arawak, then the skulls would show evidence of deformation. Arawak children had planks of wood tied to their foreheads to give them a flat backward slope that was considered a great sign of beauty by the Indians. Arawak skulls would thus have a swept-back forehead, and over-developed eyebrows. Non-Arawak skulls would be like our own, with a more vertical forehead. If we could look for this, and perhaps bring one of the skulls out for dating, it might be possible to unravel some of the mystery.

On the final dive in Sanctuary, I took a heliox tank and explored the base of Mohebi Hall. A series of broken ledges at 150 ft (45 m) led to the now familiar floor of boulders, and I squeezed among these to a final depth of 185 ft (55.5 m) – hardly worth the heliox. Collecting a few deep stalagmite samples, I made my way back out, looking longingly at the small hole that led into the unexplored north passage beneath the shotline. Then, carefully, I collected one of the skulls, and slid it into a large plastic bag brought down for the purpose. It was extremely fragile, and flakes of finer bone clouded the water in the bag as I surfaced.

In the daylight we examined it closely. Sure enough, the forehead sloped backwards at an artificially flattened angle. The remains were Arawak, and so were – at the very least – five hundred years old. Sanctuary was an important and exciting find, and one which we were determined to keep sacrosanct. The exact location of Sanctuary would (and still does) remain a secret.

CHAPTER TWELVE

Porcupine Hole

THE FINAL days of the Andros Project were a slow wind-down. With the last of the heliox used, and the end in sight, there was little impetus to explore. The winds of August blew warm rain in from the sea, and we were all beginning to feel a little physically drained after weeks of underwater work. Septic infections had hit most of those diving in the inland caves, some bacterial strain triggering a reaction in our blood-streams. I had it badly – my left foot developed an abscess at the ankle joint, which made swimming in fins increasingly painful. At length, unable to stand it any more – in fact barely able to stand at all – I pleaded with Pete Glanvill to do something.

Pete is a cave rescue doctor. That means he approaches things bluntly, in the field, at least. He filled what looked to me like a horse-syringe with penicillin and bade me bend over. I couldn't believe that such a huge amount of penicillin could be injected so quickly. Partly in slight shock, I hopped to my airbed and collapsed, speechless. But it worked. The next morning saw the two of us ferreting with fascination in the open pit, picking out lumps of green pus like errant schoolboys round a tadpole pond. I gave it a day to heal, and decided that the sea was probably safer than the sulphur layers.

We had two marine biologists working full-time out in the marine holes, Bernard Picton and Rob Trott, so Chris, Judith and I joined them for a final visit to Bidet Hole, the others intending to photograph, and me with the intention of cheating Murphy out of the bit of cave at the bottom.

I dropped two cameras off at the 50 ft (9 m) mark to pass time during decompression, and allowed a mounting inflow to carry me into the cave. I wasn't particularly concerned by the current here – I had done the same the time before, even if the flow was now a little stronger. Today I moved quickly, eager to get to the end, using fins only to give me an extra spurt of thrust when the passage size allowed. The exploration was a calculated gamble, our generators had been running roughly on contaminated petrol from the island pump and this was affecting the battery chargers. I could only depend on my 'Andros' light and one of the small Q-lites I carried; the other torches were of doubtful charge. Knowing the lie of the line through the cave was good, I felt I could risk it.

The Squeeze down through the rift to 100 ft (30 m) seemed tighter and longer, but the larger passage below soon brought me back into the big chamber and the end of the line. I hung in the hall, tracing the line of the walls by the light of my main beam. The room was about 30 ft (9 m) across and 40 ft (12 m) high, and covered with pale sponges and delicate ascidians. Flickers of movement were coral shrimps, tracking across the vertical walls like dancers out of faerie. Their eyes shone. I sank slowly through the clear dark waters to a sandy slope, and swam on down across the floor to a low squeeze at −200 ft (−60 m). Sharing the water with me as I peered through the gap was blind *Lucifuga*, the cave fish, an unexpected sight so close to the entrance of a marine cave. We sensed each other's presence in our own ways, me by sight, it by touch, my pressure waves picked up by its sensitive lateral line. With apparent indifference, it lazily turned away and went to seek out something more of a size to eat.

Three feet (0.9 m) above the Squeeze the temperature dropped, and suddenly I could see more clearly. Most likely this was simply me catching up with the last of the outflow water going back in, but it was a strange feeling all the same. I scooped through the low section, just fitting through the 2 ft (0.6 m) high gap, to pop out in another chamber, twin to the one I'd just left. The floor continued down inexorably, but the roof soared up many feet above, the walls narrowing as they went. I went up, entering warmer water again at −180 ft (−54 m). I suspected I'd missed a higher connection between the two rooms.

But the way on was down at the floor again. I dropped to the sandy slope, and moved slowly down to the base of the hall. My gauge crept round to the 230 ft (70 m) mark as the floor levelled off. I came to a stop. Two small passages with well-scoured floors led into the distance, the one on my left being far too tight to even think about attempting. Over on the right, things looked more promising, but very committing. The top of the Squeeze actually had teeth, a row of rock flakes or very corroded stalactites, and the opening looked far too like a gaping mouth for comfort. Fortunately I had too little air left for any real attempt at passing the Squeeze, but I pushed in as far as I dared all the same, and looked along a horizontal tunnel that seemed about 18 in (45 cm) high and a little over a yard (0.9 m) wide.

Next generation, I thought philosophically, tying the line emphatically to the middle tooth. With a 60 ft (18 m) stop registering on my Decobrain, it was time to go. The effort of moving against the current was greater this time, but the clarity of the water made it bearable. Rising through the two chambers was a relaxed experience, a comfortable excursion in and out of the Bahamian underworld that was, on this occasion at least, mine alone to play with. By the time I saw daylight my unhealed foot was rebelling, and I spent the next hour or so photographing the walls of the shallower cave with one fin off and one fin on while my bloodstream purged itself both of nitrogen and the poisons of the inland caves. I had plenty of time to think.

The exploration of Blue Holes has taken up much of my last seven years. It grew from the head-on beginnings of 1981, where our only impetus was the sheer adventure of exploring one of the most dangerous and spectacular frontiers left to us on Earth. Pushed by the insatiable egoism that lay in being *first,* our arrogance was matched only by the equally insatiable curiosity to see what lay beyond the limits of our lights at the end of the slender line. We grew to encompass the curiosity of *why,* a desire to learn more of the caves we swam through, of the tenuous existence of the life therein, of the aeons-old story of the caves themselves and the very rock in which they formed. We felt the timeless delight of floating in galleries of crystal wonder, silent masterpieces of natural glory in the eternal darkness of the abyss. Hidden from the day of their formation to the day of their demise, they are there until the caves collapse and destroy them, or the sands of the seas bury them in an enclosing coffin of stone.

Our exploration encompassed all this and more, an intangible sense of belonging, as if by placing our very existence on a lonely cord into the underworld and accepting the consequences, we lost man's inhibitions and his walls of indifference. Despite the sophisticated cocoon of equipment that keeps us alive, we were only creatures of the world, living parts of a living planet, cells in the naked and vulnerable body of Gaia.

For myself, in the caves, I am part of things in a way few can be. I accept that I know only part of what surrounds me, and that there is much I can never hope to know. I know that I have the ability to harm the caves beyond easy recovery, but that I would choose not to. I know enough to know that these are special places, secrets of inner space that need our understanding and love as much as the high mountains and the deep forests. They were here long before us, and there is no reason at all for them not to outlast us. They do not belong to us, but we can take on the role of guardians; we can enter them to understand them, but we can justify little more.

Mankind has come only so far – we have learned enough to be gods in an ancient world, but we shy from taking on the responsibilities of those gods. Some of those are not pleasant, and the greater balance that holds the world together sits man sometimes in one scale, sometimes another. Gaia is a demanding, impartial mistress, and it doesn't take much to fall out of her favour. We still have far to grow.

On the last day on Andros, we boated out to Porcupine Hole, a small marine hole near Kemps Bay. It was one of those days that seem fated to occur at the ends of ventures like this. This was a cave that Mary and I had seen from the air the year before, but had searched for in vain from the sea. Retrospectively, it seems almost as though this was meant to happen. Bernard and Rob came across it on a long sweep across the fault line, following it northwards to Smith's Hill, where the fracture left the sea.

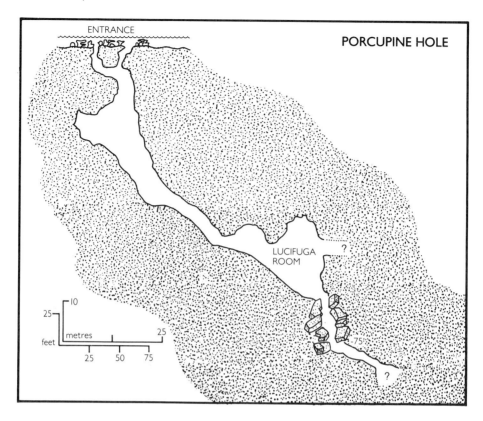

Two deep shafts lay in a small and utterly beautiful patch of reef, in less than 10 ft (3 m) of water. Corals were scattered around the mouths of the caves, not in any formal 'ring', but like an aquatic village around a desert oasis, set in pure white sands that faded into the distance in every direction. I swam into the southern opening with the last couple of hundred feet of line left from Sanctuary on my reel, not expecting wonders.

Therefore the cave came as a very pleasant surprise. Thirty feet (9 m) down, the cave opened into a cosy chamber, about 50 ft (15 m) long. In the far end, light streamed in from the northern entrance. The floor was the usual mix of bryzoans, hydroids and algal debris, a khaki, organic carpet, but the roof was ablaze with a rainbow-coloured kaleidoscope of sponges. Bernard was down at −40 ft (−12 m), taking photographs, and he gave me a friendly wave as I passed, pointing beneath his fins to a vertical rift that lay beyond their limit of exploration. He waved to the south, suggesting that the biggest passage went that way. I waved back, glancing north to check, and nodded agreement. Off I went, feet first, floating weightlessly down the crack to come to a gentle rest 130 ft (40 m) down on a sandy floor.

Levitating slightly with the aid of a blast of air, I hovered across a patch of pale bacterial matting on the sand, and passed through a low gap to emerge again into a roomy cavern 165 ft (50 m) below the surface. The roof was visible about 30 ft (9 m) above, and the sand sloped steeply down towards another wall 30 ft (9 m) below. Utterly at peace, I reached out to touch the wall, and make physical contact with the cave. My fingers traced a run of old, corroded flowstone, covered now by centuries of marine concretion and the borings of ocean wildlife. The tiny tubes of serpulid worms ran in brown whorls across the rippled surface, and delicate pink tendrils waved at their ends, filtering food from the water. I looked at the reel, knowing that it would run out of line at any moment. The last few metres spun off, and the reel jerked to a halt in my hand, only an arm's length from a beautiful belay at −190 ft (−57 m) on the far wall of the chamber. With a wry grin, I turned and found a less perfect tie-off on the west wall, a yard or so behind.

There was little opportunity to go much further without a guideline. The cave was very deep, more than I had expected, and looked like continuing so. I rose briefly in the chamber and saw that there was a narrow gap straight ahead high up in the wall, at about −150 ft (−45 m), easily large enough for side-mounts. Below the end wall, a jumble of boulders concealed a further descent. I could look vertically down a fair-sized hole, and decided to chance a look even without a line. My lights were all in order, my tolerance of narcosis was high after two months of constant deep-diving, and I felt good. A straight vertical ascent, even in low visibility, would bring me back into the chamber immediately below the line. One of the blind, white fish hovered near me as I calmly purged air from my jacket, and carefully sank down between the boulders into deeper cave. I moved with the utter slow motion of a lunar astronaut, intent on raising as little silt as possible, and sank with grace on to a sandy floor at −245 ft (−73.5 m).

Beyond lay a sloping gallery, probably 7 ft (2 m) wide, falling to a lip into darkness that probably lay at −260 ft (−78 m). Beyond, nothing could be seen, the cave swallowed up my lights, tantalizing me beyond belief. But I gazed only for a moment, beyond temptation, too aware that I had no line and my air was finite. Nor had I planned to go so deep – there was no oxygen above to decompress on. I was here under tolerance, a considerable experience had made it safe for me to do so, but at the borders of that experience were sharp and impassive boundaries. Another, smaller, *Lucifuga* shared the water with me here, a pale custodian of the cave beyond. Here was a thing – me with all my shining equipment, all my millennia of evolution from the depths of the sea, and this little creature that had stayed behind in the bowels of the planet could now go further than I. It knew what lay beyond my lights, down in the unexplored cave. It turned towards me as I knelt in the sands of the passage, and hung, unafraid of my presence, in waters I could only dream of entering.

I reached out, and pressed a button on my gear. Air screamed into my jacket from the tanks on my side, and I rose back into the murky clouds between the boulders, rising vertically through the waters to place a hand on the guideline in the chamber above. More *Lucifuga* looked silently at me as I retraced my way towards the surface, pale ghosts in the dark cavern, rippling silently in the waters of the cave. It felt as though the spirits of the caves had come to watch me depart, to remind me that this was their world, not mine.

Emerging from the underworld after the final dive in Porcupine Hole.
(Photo: Chris Howes FRPS)

I passed back into the world above, pausing in the twilight entrance hall to look fully at what would be the last Blue Hole of the Andros Project. I was selfishly glad I had explored it alone – it held everything I'd come for in its depths. The cave was utterly beautiful – soft, transluscent sponges, blue ascidians, tiny red tunicates, and an amazing array of different, delicately coloured shrimps. Cowries grazed the walls, and waving hyroids framed the brilliant blue of the entrance. I looked out, and it seemed surreal. Plains of white sand stretched away at eye level, and the sunlit waves danced ripples across its sky. A ray peered from behind a coral head, and damselfish hovered in the crevices of the entrance. Snappers and grunts and gaudy parrotfish moved through the waving gorgonians, and, somewhere in the distance, the silver flash of a baraccuda hovered on the edge of sight. I felt very content.

Slipping out of my gear in the Zodiac, I had the urge to return to the sea. Without the encumbrance of tanks and suit and the tangle of valves and gauges, I felt freer than flight. Breaking in and out of the fragile, unnecessary barrier between air and water, I spent long minutes in a joyful communion with the ocean before reluctantly returning to our world of air. The sea is only the other side of the sky.

The last ride back to base was a glorious cliche. The sea shone smooth and silver, the sun was setting, silhouetting the palms on the shore. The roar of the Mariner outboard and the bounce of the Zodiac beneath our bare feet, the warm wind of nightfall, the taste of salt and the smell of the land as we ran close to the beach touched every sense we possessed. We swept to shore under a wild sky, smiles on our lips, and it was over.

Equipment

Those of you who have made it this far may wish to know a little more about the equipment we use to explore underwater caves. What follows must in no way be taken as an instructional appendix, simply an explanation of how we go about keeping ourselves as alive as possible in what is, after all, an extremely hostile environment. If you want to learn how to actually do it (and I'd suggest there are many more pleasant ways to spend your time) then formal training from one of the national cave-diving organizations is essential.

The techniques we have used to explore Blue Holes have been a hybrid mixture of cave-diving skills developed and refined on both sides of the Atlantic. Their origin has been as often from caving as from diving sources. The successful exploration of underwater caves requires a thorough knowledge of both disciplines.

In North America, many of the techniques currently used in cave diving had their origin in Benjamin's original Blue Holes explorations. The use of lightweight line reels, and of specialist lamp units, with a waist- or tank-mounted battery-pack feeding current to a handle-held lamphead, and the conception of the 'Thirds Rule' – where one-third of the total air supply is used on the inward swim, one-third on the way out, with the last third always held in reserve in case of an emergency – came out of those days.

The extreme depth of the caves required the use of buoyancy compensating jackets – not merely life jackets, but re-inflatable vests that would allow for the diver's in-water buoyancy to be adjusted again and again throughout the course of a dive. As more fragile caves were discovered, with delicate stalagmite and stalactite galleries, careful buoyancy control became even more essential, to avoid brushing against the delicate crystal columns and bringing them crashing silently to the floor of the caves.

North American cave-divers generally wear their main tanks on their backs, linked by a dual manifold (invented by George Benjamin) that allows either of two breathing regulators access to the air in both tanks, while still allowing a faulty regulator to be isolated in an emergency.

Additional tanks are often carried, clipped to the chests of divers, to enable more distant penetration to be made. For the longest dives of all, 'air-dumps' may have to be set up in advance, extra tanks of air which are left at pre-ordained sites on the journey, to be breathed from one dump to the next like staging horses on a Pony Express ride. Each of these tanks is used in accordance to the Thirds Rule, no more than one-third being used before they are changed for another at the next staging post, and left to await a similar change-over on the way back out.

British divers favour a different system, one that has evolved from the nature of the caves they explore at home in Britain. Here, underwater cave passages are often narrow and constricted, waters are cold, and visibility is low. Tanks are worn on the diver's sides, mounted on special harnesses that keep them in place. To these harnesses, shoulder straps can be attached to make getting in and out of the water with heavy cylinders on more comfortable, and to which additional equipment can be attached – line reels, extra torches, contents gauges from each main tank, and other small items. The emphasis is on accessibility, everything should be in vision, and within easy reach. The mouthpieces are mounted on neck straps, making them instantly available when a change-over from one breathing system is required.

This may happen several times during the course of a dive. In Britain, each breathing system is self-contained, with no linking manifold. If one system fails, it is isolated completely, and the exit is immediately made on the other tank. Demand valves can be changed over underwater, but the process is not recommended, and on longer dives three tanks or more may be worn rather than staged, though staging is also used where occasion demands.

This ability to cope with 'redundant' equipment during the course of a cave dive is extended to lights and other essential gear. At least three separate light sources are carried, the primary (usually the brightest) unit, and two others. In North America, these are usually clipped to the diver's harness; in Britain, they are worn on the helmet, to provide directional light in confined spaces without encumbering hands.

Our main 12 v lighting systems on the Andros Project had been specially designed, and were built for us by Aquabeam Ltd in England. We could use either 30-watt or 100-watt lightheads with them, which made them suitable for both exploration *and* filming. Two larger 24 v units worked 250-watt heads, for when the caves got really large.

Knives, depth and contents gauges, compasses, decompression meters and a survey slate are all worn on the arms, to ease the possibility of leg entanglement, and so that they are accessible even in the most constricted of underwater passages. Most people on the Andros project used their own equipment, with which they were familiar, though we took Apeks demand valves and both Aladin and Decobrain dive computers with us.

Most cave-divers carry two line reels – one for laying down the passage they are exploring, that links them back to the surface, and another smaller one that enables them to relocate the main line should they become separated from it in low visibility, with which they can jump short gaps between lines, or with which they can make short forays from the main run. The line is all-important. If it is badly laid, entanglement or physical entrapment can occur. As silt rises from the floor of a cave, visibility can be reduced from near-perfect to absolute zero in seconds, and contact with the cord that represents the only physical guide back to the outside world is essential. Many cave divers, mostly novice, but some extremely experienced, have died simply because they could not find their way out of the cave.

In the Blue Holes, we mainly used 3,000 psi, 80 cu. ft (6.8 cu. m) aluminium air tanks, supplied by Luxfer. American divers brought their steel 'double-hundreds'. These back-mounted 2,000 psi, 100 cu. ft (8.5 cu. m) bottles are over-pumped somewhat to provide as much air as possible. We also used lightweight composite tanks, made by Acurex, which had a much higher working pressure of 4,500 psi, and which held 105 cu. ft (8.9 cu. m) when slightly over-pumped. These, made from aluminium tightly bound with kevlar fibre, were extremely lightweight and easy to carry, but for which the diver paid an extra penalty in lead weight, as they were considerably more buoyant than the other tanks.

For the deepest dives, we wore DUI or Viking drysuits, both for their thermal advantages and as a secondary inflation system. On deep SCUBA dives, where the breathing gas was definitely finite, the suits were worn under buoyancy compensators, in case a rip in either inflation system trapped the diver on the bottom at great depth. This could have been as fatal an accident as a total gas failure. Undersuits of Thinsulate material were worn. Most diving was done in wetsuits, specially made for us by Warmbac Ltd in England.

The rebreathers

The rebreathers were undoubtedly the most exciting of the equipment used during the Andros Project, and point the way towards the deep and distant underwater cave explorations of the future.

The systems we used on Andros were essentially Rexnord Mark 16 units, modified by Carmellan for use on short-duration excursions to great depth. Using a slightly higher partial pressure of oxygen in the breathing mixture than in ordinary air (which would be lethal for long dives) meant that short spells could be spent down to 700 ft (210 m) with correspondingly shorter in-water decompressions. We were cleared to use the units to 500 ft (150 m) if the caves went that deep, though as it turned out the 320 ft (96 m) depth attained in Stargate was the deepest we got.

The original idea had been to use an experimental mixture of neon and oxygen (neox) for the dives, but the budget did not allow this and we reverted to heliox (a mixture of helium and oxygen). Though we trusted the rebreathers implicitly, and had no real in-water problems, we always carried a bail-out tanks of heliox with a 20 per cent oxygen/80 per cent helium mix in it. This, suitable for breathing at depths of up to 300 ft (90 m) or so, would allow us to retreat to a shallower depth and regain the entrance, down which hung an umbilical with two separate demand valves as a safety cover. The umbilical was linked to a 'J' cylinder of oxygen at the surface, with an ordinary diving tank acting as a 'holding tank' attached to the demand valves at the other end, to enable surface tanks to be changed over without interrupting the supply to the divers. All the decompression was done in the water, using the rebreathers to -30 ft (-9 m), and there changing over to pure oxygen fed down the umbilical.

An inflatable recompression chamber was kept at base, and portable oxygen/intravenous drip sets were kept at the surface in case of decompression sickness. Evacuation to a therapeutic recompression chamber on North Andros, at the AUTEC base, and from there in extreme emergency to the US Navy base in Panama City, North Florida, had been arranged, and we felt we could have a casualty helicoptered to AUTEC within the hour if things had gone badly wrong. Fortunately, nothing did.

The emergency inflatable recompression chamber being tested. *(Photo: Rob Parker)*

It says much for the application and dedication of those involved that such a high number of deep air and helium dives were made in previously unexplored caves over such a short time, in such arduous surface conditions (thick jungle, 90° F (33° C) heat) and remote locations, and no one got hurt. Theoretically, the odds had been set against that. You can never be careful enough.

Sponsorship

The Andros Project was supported by a great number of companies and individuals on both sides of the Atlantic, and it is only through this generous support that it was possible to mount the Project in the first place. Too often, this assistance goes unrecognized, but we would like to make it known that the individuals and organizations who contributed so much to the venture are every bit as responsible for the success of the Andros Project as are those who had the good fortune to be at the 'sharp end'. Our heartfelt thanks go to all those listed below, and to all those others who contributed in any way to the success of the venture.

AEM Ltd
Air Products
Amatek Ltd
Ansa Software
Apeks Marine
Aquabeam Ltd
Bahamas National Trust
Bahamasair
E.P. Barrus Ltd
Benjamin Film Laboratories
Berghaus Ltd
Bishop Lifting Services
British Airways Cargo Division
British Sport Council
Camera Care Systems
Carmellan Research Ltd
Cavalier Shipping Ltd
Compaq Computers
Cunard Brocklebank
Deep Ocean Systems
Diving Unlimited
Eastern Airlines
Gemini Graphics
Ghar Parau Foundation
Haskel Ltd
Hogg Robinson/Gardner Mountain
    Marine
Hogg Robinson Travel
Honda UK Ltd
Honeywell Italia Ltd
Hyett Adams Ltd
Jerry's Honk 'n Holler
Kentmere Ltd
Luxfer Ltd

Lyon Equipment
Mako Compressors
MicroPro International
MP United Drug Co Ltd
National Environmental Research
  Council
National Geographic Television
Navstar Ltd
Nikon UK
Paterson Ltd
Photo Technology
Rolex (International) Ltd
Royal Geographical Society
Safety Air Services

Sea and Sea Ltd (UK)
Shell (Bahamas) Ltd
Shell (Exploration) PLC
SOS (UK) Ltd
Spirotechnique UK Ltd
Sub Sea Services
Tower Scaffolding Ltd
Varta UK Ltd
Virgin Divers World
Warmbac Ltd
Zainal Mohebi and the Mohebi
  Group of Companies Ltd
Zodiac UK

In the Bahamas: Ministry of Agriculture and Local Government, Department of Lands and Surveys, Ministry of Works, British High Commission, Forfar Field Station, Colin Higgs, John Hook, Richard Cant, Gary and Susan Larsen, Godfrey 'Tippy' Lightbourne, Steve and Liz Haddock and the Bahamas Dive Club, Stan and Dorothy Clarke, Norbert Rahming, Neil Sealey, Joy Chaplin, Cdr Ian Anderson-Mochrie, RN, Dennis and Anne Carliss, Small Hope Bay Lodge, Bahamas National Trust

In the UK: Dr Nic Fleming, Surgeon Admiral Sir John Rawlins, Dr Maurice Cross, John Bevan, Robin Turner, Andrew Wilkie, Don Rodocker

In the USA: Wes and Terri Skiles, Lester Cole, David and Hannah Pincus, Roberta Swicegood, Tom Davies, Jerry Nelson

In Canada: Dr George Benjamin, Hanni Benjamin, George Benjamin Jnr, Chris Benjamin, Peter Benjamin, Tom McCollum

TEAM MEMBERS
Rob Palmer   Director and deep diving team
Ian Bishop   Deputy director and logistics manager
Dr Peter Smart   Geologist and hydrologist, diver
Dr John Mylroie   Geologist
Dr James Carew   Geologist
Dr Bill Stone   Deep diving team
Dr David Whiteside   Sedimentologist
Dr Peter Glanvill   Medical officer, cave diver
Rob Parker   Deep diving team
Richard Stevenson   Cave diver and electronics manager
Fiona Whittaker   Hydrologist and diver
Bernard Picton   Marine biologist, diver
Robert Trott   Marine biologist, diver
Brad Pecel   Cave diver
Pat Stone   Diving and base camp support
John Hutchinson   Terrestial biologist
Paul Steward   Terrestial biologist
Chris Howes   Photographer, diver
Judith Calford   Diver, photographic assistant
Ian Kelly   Base camp manager
Stuart Clough   Carmellan Research, deep-diving team
Neil Cave   Carmellan Research, deep-diving team
Bill Hamilton   Carmellan Research
Sharon Yskamp   Carmellan Research

Film crew
Sarah Cunliffe   Director, Oxford Scientific Films
Paul Atkins   Camerman, Moana Productions
Grace Niska   Sound recordist, Moana Productions
Keith Turner   Assistant camerman, Moana Productions

1986 reconnaissance
Rob Palmer
Dr Peter Smart
Mary Stafford Smith
Sue Wells
Fiona Whittaker

Index

Black and white illustrations are given in bold, colour plates in roman.

Andros **10, 17, 21**
  boat building 14–15
  description of 14–15
  island name 14
  Project, conception of 78
  west coast of 44–5
Andros, Sir Edmund 14
Arawaks 55–6, 140–2
  annihilation by Spaniards 141
  bones in Sanctuary (XII) 140–2
  creation legends 141
  remains in caves 118, 140–2
Archie's Blue Hole 46–8
Atkins, Paul **98**, 107, **109**, 113
AUTEC recompression chamber 84, 154, **154**
Avalon Blue Hole 93–5, **94**

Bahamas, formation of 21–3
Base Camp, description of 90
Beaumont, Rod 40, 42, 48–9
Benjamin, Dr George xii, 1–2, 5–14, **16**, 18–34, 36–7, 41–2, 43, 45–7, 55, 65, 139, 151, 152
Benjamin, George Jnr xii, **16**, 19, 20, 37
Benjamin, Hanni xii
Benjamin's Blue Hole (SB4) 24, **24, 26**, 78
  deaths in 30, 31, **31**
  discovery of (II) 27
  exploration of 24–31, **31**

Bidet Hole 134–5, **135**, 143–5
Birch, Dick 18, 19, 65
Birch, Jack 13
Birch, Rosie 65
Bishop, Ian ('Bish') 85, 88–91, **98**, 122, 128
Black Hole (III)
Blashford-Snell, John 74–5
Blue Holes xi, **10, 21**
  fauna of (VI) 79–80
  formation of 21–3
  inland 44–5
Bolliner, Heinz 7–8, 9, 19, 37
Boycott, Tony 69–71

Calford, Judith 85, 87, **98**, 126, 132, 143
Captain Moxey **87**
Carcelle, John 30, 32
Carew, Jim **98**
Carmellan research 82–3, 97, 123, 126
Cat Island 74
Cave, Neil 83, **98**, 99, 100, 122
Chapman, Roger 74
Chickcharnies 46
  curse 12
  disappearance of 18
  fossil nest sites 114, 129
  giant owls 45, 114, 129
Clarke, Dorothy 58, 60, 89
Clarke, Stan 58–9, 60, 89

Clough, Stuart (XI) 82, **83**, 97, **98**, 99, 100, 106–8, **109**, 110, 119, 122
Columbus, Bahamian 'discovery' 141
Conch Sound Blue Hole (IV) **17**, 35–6, **38–9**, **40–1**, **68**
  1981 explorations 37–43, 85
  1982 explorations 56, 61–3, 66–72, 91
  Benjamin's explorations 12–13, 36–7
Conch Sound Two 43, 49
Coral Hole 57, 78
Cousteau, Jacques 19, 25, 55
Cousteau, Philippe 27
Cross, Dr Morris 82, 83
Cunliffe, Sarah 97, **98**, 122
currents, reversing 79

Dangerous Brothers 128
decompression 10–11, 30, 126, 128, 138, 140
  Carmellan tables 83, 123
  computer profiles 108–9, **109**, 122, 128
  facilities on Andros 152–3
  one-man recompression chamber 84
Deep Creek, Blue Holes (V) **17**, 56, 85
deep-diving, research into 81
Diving Diseases Research Centre 82, 83, **83**

Easegill Caverns, discovery of 20
El Dorado (VII) **115**
  1987 explorations 114–19, 121–3
  bottomed 126–9
  discovery of 114
Elvenhome **103**
  exploration of 103–6, 132
Exley, Sheck 33, 81, 99–100, 122

Fairclough, Isobel **98**
Falco 25
Farr, Martyn xii, 3, 4, 38–9, 41, 42, 48–51, 56, 64–74, **68**
Faulkner, Douglas 19
Forfar, Archie 5, 6, 8–10, 33, 37, 45
Forfar Field Station 2, 46, 51, 53, 66
Fort Bovisand 82, 83, **83**, 109, 121
freshwater lens 46, 79

Gaia 145
Gibbins, Duncan 62, 66, 67, 69, 70
Glanvill, Peter 98, 130, 132, 138, 143
Great Bahama Bank 16, **17**

Hamilton, Dr Bill 83, 98, 108–11, **109**
Hardington, Gary 75–6
Hartlebury, Bob 75–7
Hasenmayer, Jochen 81
Haskel Boost Pump 91, **115**
  arrival of 98–9
Hatt, Pete 75–6
Heron Hole **103**, 105
Howes, Chris xii, 85–9, **98**, 126, 143
Hutchins, Roger 19
Hutchison, John (V) **98**
hutia 114, 129

Ice Ages 18, 22, 137
Ikehara, Ike 27
Iliffe, Tom 112

Jellyfish Lake 80
  exploration of 113–14, 128
  'Swimming Hole' 113–14
Johnson, 'Captain' Joe 13, 14
Johnson, Ivan 13
Jones, Ken and Laurie 2, 46, 51–2, 66

Kelly, Ian ('Yanto') 91, **98**, 108, 122, 123, 126, 128

Lightbourne, 'Tippy' 98
Lighthouse Reef Blue Hole 25
lighting equipment, underwater 9–10, 91, 107, 151, 152
Loach, Paul de 100
Lockwood, Jim 30, 31, **31**, 32
Lucayan Cavern 140
Lucifuga cave fish 3, 51, 72, 80, 129, 144, 147
Lusca 12, 35–6, 37, 39, 42

McCollum, Carol 13
McCollum, Mike 13, 36
McInnis, Joe 19
Madden, Mike 114, 121, 124
mail boat 86

Mangrove Cay
   blue holes 7–11, 20, 21, 23, 33
   island of 5–7, 14
Mars Bay Blue Hole 59, 60, 99–100
Martz, Frank 27, 30–3, **31**
Mays, Colin 134, 136, **136**
Mays, Nick 134, 136
mixing zone 47, 139
Mohebi, Zainal 132
Mohebi Hall (XIII) **131**, 132–3, 137, 138, 140, 141
Mount, Tom 25–7, 29, 31, 32
MV *Victoria* 56, 58
Mylroie, John **98**, 108

narcosis, influence of 19–20, 30, 117, 119, 123
NERC deep diving project 97
Nicolls Town 61, 66
Niska, Grace **98**
North Bight Blue Hole 13, **17**

Operation Raleigh 74, 75, 78, 80, 101

Parker, Rob (XI) 56, 60, 62–4, 66, 69, 71–3, 83, **83**, 91–2, 97, **98**, 99–100, 105, 106, **109**, 110–11, 119–20, **120**, 122, 145
Pecel, Brad **98**, 106, 108, 127
Phantom 500 ROV, underwater vehicle 84, **113**
photography, underwater 6
Picton, Bernard (XIII) 98, 143, 145, 146
Pimlock, Jane 82
Plummer, Liz 58, 61
Porcupine Hole (XIV) 145–9, **146**, **148**
Project Andros, US expedition 113–14

Rat Bat Cave 114
Rat Bat Lake, link with El Dorado 114, **115**, 121
Ray Cay
   blue hole (I, XVI) 2–4
   island of 1, 13
rebreathers 81, **83**, 100, 106–11, 114, 119, **120**, 121, 122, 153–5
   Carmellan 82–3, 92, 111, 153

early models 82–3
   Rexnord Mk 16 153
Remipedia 80, 137
   Godzillius 137

Sanctuary (XII) 130–42, **131**, **136**
   bottomed 136–9
   discovery of 131
Sarvary, Anne 58, 61
School Hole 93, 101–5, **103**
Scoones, Peter 70
Sealey, Neil 141
Shark Hole (III) 134
Shaw, Jenny 75
Shell Exploration 97
Singer, Betty 13, 19
Small Hope Bay 18, 65, 106
Smart, Peter 78, 79, 97, **98**, 110, 111, 122, 125, 126
snakes
   boa constrictor 114
   brown racer 91
South Bight **17**
   blue holes (II) 23, 28–9, 33, 78
   SB2 23, 28
Spellar, Mike 91
Stafford Smith, Mary 77, 78, 134, 145
Stargate (IX, XI) 76, 77, **113**, 116, **120**, **124**
   bottomed 120–6
   discovery of 75–8, 101
   exploration of 81–4, 92, 106–9, 113, 119–26, 137
   rebreathers in 81–4
   US expedition 113
Stevenson, Richard (X) 91–2, 96, **98**, 105, 121, 123–5
Stone, Bill (VII) xii, 90–2, 97–100, **98**, 105, 114, **115**, 116–19, 122–3, 127–8
Stone, Pat 90–1, **98**, 112, 126
Swicegood, Roberta 98

Tomorrow's World 82
Tongue of the Ocean 16, **17**, 43, 46, 55, 56–8
   formation of 22
Treco, Harry 62

Trott, Rob 98, 143
Turner, Dana 99
Turner, Keith **98**, **109**, **113**
Turner, Parker 113, 114

Uncle Charlie's Blue Hole 51–2, **53**
'Unicorn', cave creature 80

Vinall, Mark 101–4

Walker, Julian 56, 57–8, 62–4, 66, 70,
    71, 73
'Wall', The 11, 18
    Archie Forfar's death 33
    diving 19–20, 33, 54–5
Warner, George 40

Waterman, Stan 33
Wells, Sue 78
Werner, Roger 121, 124
Westcob, Alan 94
Whiteside, Dave **98**
Whittaker, Fiona 78, 91–2, **98** 105,
    119, 123
Williams, Dennis 112–13, 114, 121
Williams, Dick 25, 26

Yanto *see* Kelly, Ian
Yskamp, Sharon **98**, **109**
Yucatan, *cenotes* 47

Zidi 32
Zumrick, John 100